Daily Academic Vocabulary

GRADE 2

All illustrations and photography, including those from Shutterstock.com, are protected by copyright.

Editorial
Development: Bonnie Brook Communications
Content Editing: Marilyn Evans
Leslie Sorg
Copy Editing: Sonny Bennett
Art Direction: Cheryl Puckett
Cover Design: Cheryl Puckett
Illustration: Jim Palmer
Design/Production: Carolina Caird

EMC 2758
Visit
teaching-standards.com
to view a correlation
of this book.

Correlated to Current Standards

Congratulations on your purchase of some of the finest teaching materials in the world.

Photocopying the pages in this book is permitted for <u>single-classroom use only</u>. Making photocopies for additional classes or schools is prohibited.

For information about other Evan-Moor products, call 1-800-777-4362, fax 1-800-777-4332, or visit our website, www.evan-moor.com. Entire contents © 2007 Evan-Moor Corporation 10 Harris Court, Suite C-3, Monterey, CA 93940-5773. Printed in USA.

CPSIA: P.A. Hutchison Co., Mayfield, PA, USA [2/2024]

Contents

WEEK		PAGE
1	fact, opinion, test	10
2	important, importance, main, minor	14
3	common, in common, uncommon, special	18
4	equal, alike, unlike	22
5	combine, combination, connect, connection	26
6	correct, correction	30
7	explain, example	34
8	agree, agreement, disagree	38
9	review of weeks 1–8	42
10	list, item, group	46
11	choose, choice	50
12	appear, appearance	54
13	image, imagine, imagination, imaginary	58
14	invent, invention, create, creation	62
15	solve, solution, figure, figure out	66
16	amount, measure, measures, measurement	70
17	improve, improvement, success, successful	74
18	review of weeks 10–17	78
19	different, similar, compare, comparison	82

WEEK		PAGE
20	place, replace, remove	86
21	record, result	90
22	reply, report	94
23	know, knowledge	98
24	believe, belief, clue, hint	102
25	direct, indirect, direction, directions	106
26	pattern, copy, trace	110
27	**review of weeks 19–26**	114
28	state, statement, restate	118
29	plan, prepare	122
30	observe, observation	126
31	position, locate, located, location	130
32	complete, completely, completion	134
33	gather, collect, collection	138
34	examine, study	142
35	rule, require, requirement	146
36	**review of weeks 28–35**	150

Answer Key 154

Word Index 159

Reproducible Definitions 160

About Academic Vocabulary

What Is Academic Vocabulary?

Academic vocabulary is that critical vocabulary that students meet again and again in their reading and classroom work across all content areas. Feldman and Kinsella refer to these high-use, widely applicable words—words such as *compare, occurrence, structure, sequential, symbolize,* and *inference*—as "academic tool kit words."[1]

Why Is Academic Vocabulary Instruction Important?

Vocabulary knowledge is one of the most reliable predictors of academic success. Studies show a major difference over time between the achievement levels of children who enter school with a strong oral vocabulary and those who begin their schooling with a limited vocabulary. Dr. Anita Archer says, "In many ways the 'Reading Gap,' especially after second and third grades, is essentially a Vocabulary Gap—and the longer students are in school the wider the gap becomes."[2] Focused vocabulary instruction can reduce this gap.

Knowing academic vocabulary—the "vocabulary of learning"—is essential for students to understand concepts presented in school. Yet academic English is not typically part of students' natural language and must be taught. "One of the most crucial services that teachers can provide, particularly for students who do not come from academically advantaged backgrounds, is systematic instruction in important academic terms."[3]

What Does Research Say About Vocabulary Instruction?

Common practices for teaching vocabulary—looking up words in the dictionary, drawing meaning from context, and impromptu instruction—are important but cannot be depended upon alone to develop the language students need for academic success.

Most vocabulary experts recommend a comprehensive vocabulary development program with direct instruction of important words. *Daily Academic Vocabulary* utilizes direct teaching in which students use academic language in speaking, listening, reading, and writing. Used consistently, *Daily Academic Vocabulary* will help students acquire the robust vocabulary necessary for academic success.

---

[1] Feldman, K., and Kinsella, K. "Narrowing the Language Gap: The Case for Explicit Vocabulary Instruction." New York: Scholastic, 2004.
[2] Archer, A. "Vocabulary Development." Working paper, 2003. (http://www.fcoe.net/ela/pdf/Anita%20Archer031.pdf)
[3] Marzano, R. J. and Pickering, D. J. *Building Academic Vocabulary*. Alexandria, VA: Association for Supervision and Curriculum Development, 2005.

Tips for Successful Vocabulary Teaching

The "Weekly Walk-Through" on pages 6 and 7 presents a suggested instructional path for teaching the words in *Daily Academic Vocabulary*. Here are some ideas from vocabulary experts to ensure that students get the most from these daily lessons.*

Active Participation Techniques

- Active participation means ALL students are speaking and writing.
- Use **choral responses**:
    - Pronounce the word together.
    - Read the sentence/question together.
    - Complete cloze sentences together.
- Use **nonverbal responses**:
    - Students give thumbs-up signal, point to the word, etc.
    - Make sure students wait for your signal to respond.
- Use **partner responses**:
    - Have students practice with a partner first.
    - Listen in on several pairs.
- Allow thinking time before taking responses.
- Randomly call on students; don't ask for raised hands.
- Ask students to rephrase what a partner or other classmate said.

Model and Practice

- Use an oral cloze strategy when discussing a new word. Invite choral responses. For example: *If I read you the end of a story, I am reading you the ___.* (Students say, "conclusion.")
- Complete the open-ended sentence (activity 1 on Days 1–4) yourself before asking students to do so.
- Make a point of using the week's words in your conversation and instruction (both oral and written). Be sure to call students' attention to the words and confirm understanding in each new context.
- Encourage students to look for the week's words as they read content area texts.
- Find moments during the day (waiting in line, in between lessons) to give students additional opportunities to interact with the words. For example:

    *If what I say is an example of **accomplish**, say "accomplish." If what I say is <u>not</u> an example of **accomplish**, show me a thumbs-down sign.*

    I meant to clean my room, but I watched TV instead. (thumbs down)
    Stacia read two books a week, more than any other student. ("accomplish")
    The scientists found a cure for the disease. ("accomplish")
    The mechanic could not fix our car. (thumbs down)

* See also page 9 for specific ideas for English language learners.

Weekly Walk-Through

Each week of *Daily Academic Vocabulary* follows the same five-day format, making the content more accessible for both students and teacher.

Using the reproducible definitions and the teacher lesson plan page, follow the instructional steps below to introduce each day's word or words.

1. **Pronounce** the word and point out the part of speech. Then have students say the word with you several times. If the word is long, pronounce it again by syllables, having students repeat after you.

2. **Read the definition** of the word; paraphrase using simpler or different language if necessary.

3. **Read the example sentence** and then have students read it with you. Discuss how the word is used in the sentence and ask questions to confirm understanding. For example: *We are waiting for a **definite** answer from Aunt Caitlin about when she is coming for a visit.* Ask: *What kind of answer would be a **definite** answer? What kind of answer would not be a **definite** answer?* Provide additional example sentences as necessary.

4. **Elaborate** on the meaning of the word using the suggestions on the teacher lesson plan page. These suggestions draw on common life experiences to illustrate the word meaning and give students opportunities to generate their own examples of use.

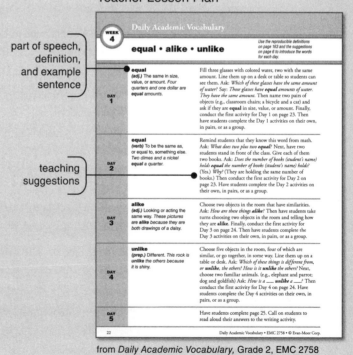

from *Daily Academic Vocabulary*, Grade 2, EMC 2758

Student Practice Pages

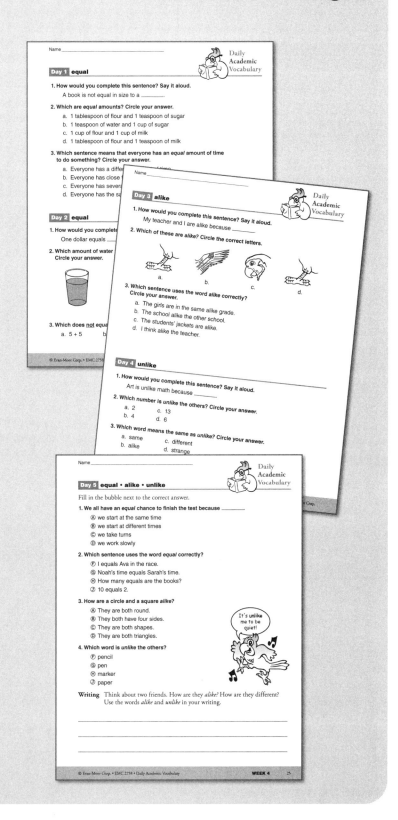

5. **Assess** students' understanding of the word(s) with the reproducible activities for Days 1 through 4.

   The first item is always an oral activity that is designed to be open-ended and answerable based on personal experience. You may wish to model a response before asking students to complete the item. Make sure that all students respond orally. Then call on a number of students to share their responses or those of a partner.

   Until students become familiar with the variety of formats used in the daily practice, you may wish to do the activities together as a class. This will provide support for English language learners and struggling readers.

6. **Review and assess** mastery of all the words from the week on Day 5. The review contains four multiple-choice items and a writing activity requiring students to use one or more of the week's words.

The instructional steps above were modeled after those presented by Kevin Feldman, Ed.D. and Kate Kinsella, Ed.D. in "Narrowing the Language Gap: The Case for Explicit Vocabulary Instruction," Scholastic Inc., 2004.

© Evan-Moor Corporation • EMC 2758 • Daily Academic Vocabulary

Review Week Walk-Through

Weeks 9, 18, 27, and 36 are review weeks. Each review covers all the words from the previous eight weeks.

Days 1–4

On Day 1 through Day 4 of the review weeks, students determine which academic vocabulary words complete a cloze paragraph.

Day 5

Day 5 of the review weeks alternates between a crossword puzzle and a crack-the-code puzzle.

Teacher Page

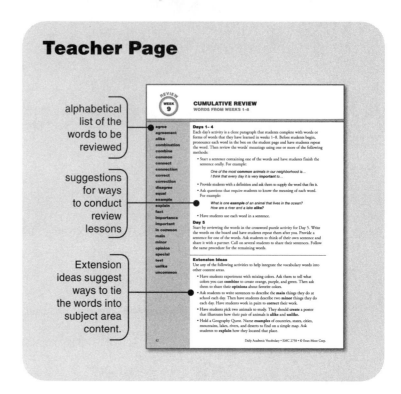

- alphabetical list of the words to be reviewed
- suggestions for ways to conduct review lessons
- Extension ideas suggest ways to tie the words into subject area content.

Student Reproducibles

Days 1–4   **Day 5**

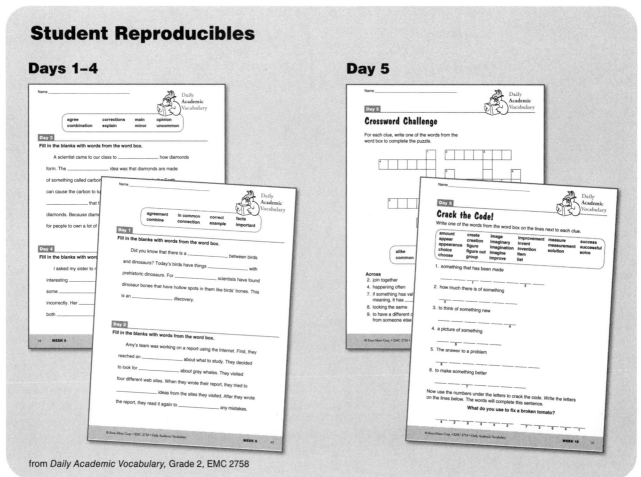

from *Daily Academic Vocabulary*, Grade 2, EMC 2758

Meeting the Needs of English Language Learners

In addition to the direct, scaffolded instruction presented in *Daily Academic Vocabulary*, you may want to use some of the following sheltering strategies to assist English language learners in accessing the vocabulary.

Use Graphics
Draw a picture, a symbol, or other graphics such as word or idea maps to represent the word. Keep it simple. Then ask students to draw their own pictures. For example:

Use Cognates with Spanish-Speaking Students
Cognates—words that are similar in meaning, spelling, and pronunciation—can make English more accessible for Spanish speakers. There are thousands of English words that have a related Spanish word. For example:

typical	típico
variety	variedad
combination	combinación

Model Correct Syntax and Usage in Oral Discussions
Model correct pronunciation. Use echoing strategies to teach correct usage and syntax. Teach the varied forms of words together, *agree* and *agreement* for example, to help students understand correct usage.

Provide Sentence Frames
For written activities, such as the final activity on all Day 5 pages, provide sentence starters or sentence frames that students can complete. For example:

*We knew that our study method was **effective** because...*

Teach Communication Strategies
Engaging in academic discussions requires a more formal language. Teach a variety of ways to begin responses when reporting or asking questions in class. For example:

Change this	To this
My partner said...	My partner shared/pointed out/indicated that...
That's not right!	I don't agree with you because...
I don't get it.	Will you explain that to me again?

Daily Academic Vocabulary

WEEK 1

fact • opinion • test

Use the reproducible definitions on page 160 and the suggestions on page 6 to introduce the words for each day.

DAY 1

fact
(noun) Something that is known to be true or to have really happened. *It's a **fact** that there are twelve months in a year.*

Say these sentences aloud and have students raise their hands if the statements are true: *We go to school during the week. We live on the planet Earth.* Tell students that a statement that is true or that describes something that really happened is a **fact**. Then have volunteers suggest other **facts**, for example, the day's weather or the number of students in class. Finally, conduct the first activity for Day 1 on page 11. Then have students complete the Day 1 activities on their own, in pairs, or as a group.

DAY 2

opinion
(noun) A belief or idea about something. *In my **opinion**, ice cream is the best dessert.*

Say: *I think that red is the best color.* Then ask: *Is this statement a fact or an **opinion**?* Say: *If a statement cannot be proven to be true or if it is something that someone believes, then it is an **opinion**.* Words such as "best," "think," "believe," "probably," and "worst" are clue words that a statement is an **opinion**. Have students offer examples of **opinions** having to do with sports. They could use sentence starters such as, "The best sport is ___" or "In my **opinion**, ___." Then conduct the first activity for Day 2 on page 11. Have students complete the Day 2 activities on their own, in pairs, or as a group.

DAY 3

test
(verb) To try something out in order to judge it or to find out more about it. *I sat on the bike and **tested** the height to see if it was the right size for me.*

Display an electric fan or some other electrical device. Ask: *How would I **test** this to see if it is working today?* Then display a soccer ball or basketball. Ask: *How would I **test** this to see if it has enough air in it to play ball?* Have students use the word **test** in their responses. Finally, conduct the first activity for Day 3 on page 12. Have students complete the Day 3 activities on their own, in pairs, or as a group.

DAY 4

test
(noun) A set of questions to find out how much someone knows about something. *We had a surprise **test** on our number facts this morning.*

Display a sample student **test**. Ask: *What kind of **test** is this?* Follow up by asking: *What other kinds of **tests** have you taken? Why do you think teachers give **tests**?* Then conduct the first activity for Day 4 on page 12. Have students complete the Day 4 activities on their own, in pairs, or as a group.

DAY 5

Have students complete page 13. Call on students to read aloud their answers to the writing activity.

Name_____

Day 1 fact

1. How would you complete this sentence? Say it aloud.

   It is a fact that our school is _tortur_.

2. Which one best completes this sentence? Circle your answer.

   A *fact* is something that _____.

   (a.) is true
   b. is false
   c. can be proven
   d. cannot be proven

3. Which sentence states a *fact*? Circle your answer.

   a. Parrots are the best animals.
   (b.) Parrots have four toes on each foot.
   c. Parrots are funny.
   d. Parrots are the most beautiful birds of all.

Day 2 opinion

1. How would you complete this sentence? Say it aloud.

   In my opinion, school lunches are _disgusting_.

2. How would you complete this sentence to form an *opinion*? Circle your answer.

   A seesaw _____.

   a. is a long board
   b. goes up at one end and down at the other
   c. needs two people to work
   d. is fun to ride

3. Which of these sentences state an *opinion*? Circle your answers.

   a. Frog and Toad Together is the best story in the world.
   b. Everyone should read Frog and Toad Together.
   c. Frog and Toad Together was written by Arnold Lobel.
   d. Frog and Toad Together was written in 1971.

Name_____

Daily Academic Vocabulary

Day 3 test

1. **How would you complete this sentence? Say it aloud.**

    One reason new toys are tested before they are sold is _____.

2. **How would you *test* a food to see if you like it? Circle your answer.**

    a. Throw it away.
    b. Give it to your friend.
    c. Taste a small bite.
    d. Touch it.

3. **Which question would *test* whether you had read a story? Circle your answer.**

    a. What is this story mainly about?
    b. Who wrote this story?
    c. Where did you find this story?
    d. How many stories have you read today?

Day 4 test

1. **How would you complete this sentence? Say it aloud.**

    When you take a test, you should _____.

2. **What kind of *test* would you take to see if you could add? Circle your answer.**

    a. spelling
    b. history
    c. reading
    d. math

3. **Which sentence uses *test* correctly? Circle your answer.**

    a. I took a spelling test today.
    b. I sharpened my pencil test.
    c. The best test I got was an A.
    d. The test of that book is hard to read.

12 **WEEK 1**   Daily Academic Vocabulary • EMC 2758 • © Evan-Moor Corporation

Name _____

4/23

Daily Academic Vocabulary

Day 5 fact • opinion • test

Fill in the bubble next to the correct answer.

1. It is a *fact* that _____.
- Ⓐ libraries have many kinds of books
- Ⓑ books are hard to find in a library
- Ⓒ libraries are the only places to go to find books
- Ⓓ libraries are the best places to go after school

2. Which sentence states an *opinion*?
- Ⓕ A soccer ball is bigger than a baseball.
- Ⓖ In soccer, you use your feet and not your hands.
- Ⓗ The goalie has the hardest job to do.
- Ⓙ Soccer is played by two teams.

3. How would you *test* spelling skills?
- Ⓐ Have students subtract numbers.
- Ⓑ Have students spell words.
- Ⓒ Have students read a story.
- Ⓓ Have students run a race.

4. What kind of *test* could a doctor give you?
- Ⓕ a driving test
- Ⓖ a math test
- Ⓗ a cooking test
- Ⓙ an eye test

Writing Think about your school. Write one *fact* about your school. Then write one *opinion*. Use the words *fact* and *opinion* in your sentences.

_____

_____

_____

Daily Academic Vocabulary

WEEK 2

important • importance
main • minor

Use the reproducible definitions on page 161 and the suggestions on page 6 to introduce the words for each day.

DAY 1

important
(adj.) Having great value, meaning, or influence. *Learning to spell is **important**.*

Ask: *What is **important** to do each day?* (e.g., eat breakfast; do your homework) Then ask: *What things are **important** to have in your life?* (e.g., family and friends) *Why are those things **important**?* Finally, conduct the first activity for Day 1 on page 15. Then have students complete the Day 1 activities on their own, in pairs, or in a group.

DAY 2

importance
(noun) The condition of being important. *The dentist told us about the **importance** of brushing our teeth.*

Display some important objects in the classroom, such as textbooks, a dictionary, and a pencil. Hold up each one and ask: *What is the **importance** of this object?* Then have students complete the following sentences aloud. Ask: *What is the **importance** of family?* Discuss responses. Then ask: *What is the **importance** of friends?* Then conduct the first activity for Day 2 on page 15. Have students complete the Day 2 activities on their own, in pairs, or as a group.

DAY 3

main
(adj.) Most important. *The **main** idea of the book is that friendships are valuable.*

Remind students that they know this word from reading when they identify the **main** idea, or the most important idea. Ask: *What is the **main** thing you do at school?* Then ask: *What are the **main** parts of your body? In other words, what parts do you think are most important?* Encourage students to use the word **main** in their responses. Then conduct the first activity for Day 3 on page 16. Have students complete the Day 3 activities on their own, in pairs, or as a group.

DAY 4

minor
(adj.) Small in importance or size. *The actor had a **minor** part in the play and only appeared once.*

Explain that if something is **minor**, it isn't very important or doesn't matter very much. Have students point to objects in the classroom they think are **minor** in either size or importance. Ask: *Why is this a **minor** part of the classroom?* Choose a story or book students have recently read and have them identify the **minor** characters. Then conduct the first activity for Day 4 on page 16. Have students complete the Day 4 activities on their own, in pairs, or as a group.

DAY 5

Have students complete page 17. Call on students to read aloud their answers to the writing activity.

Name_____

Day 1 important

1. How would you complete this sentence? Say it aloud.

   _____ is an important person in my life because _____.

2. What are two *important* things to know about school?
   Circle your answers.

   a. what time school begins   c. TV shows

   b. popular music   d. where your classroom is

3. What is *important* to remember about a story?
   Circle your answers.

   a. the characters   c. what happens

   b. the color of the words   d. the size of the words

Day 2 importance

1. How would you complete this sentence? Say it aloud.

   The importance of going to school is _____.

2. Which sentence shows the *importance* of water?
   Circle your answer.

   a. Water is found in lakes and streams.

   b. Water is wet.

   c. Water helps plants grow.

   d. Water falls as rain, hail, or snow.

3. What is the *importance* of studying for a test?
   Circle your answer.

   a. You spend a lot of time doing it.

   b. You learn things that help you answer questions.

   c. Studying keeps you quiet.

   d. Everyone knows how to study.

Name_____

Day 3 main

1. How would you complete this sentence? Say it aloud.

    In the last story I read, the main character is _____.

2. What is the *main* idea of the last story you read?

    _____

    _____

3. What are two *main* parts of a bicycle? Circle your answers.

  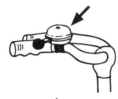   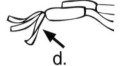

   a.   b.   c.   d.

Day 4 minor

1. How would you complete this sentence? Say it aloud.

    I think a minor ingredient in a sandwich is _____.

2. Which one is a *minor* part of a car? Circle your answer.

    a. steering wheel
    b. arm rest
    c. engine
    d. four tires

3. Which sentence uses *minor* correctly? Circle your answer.

    a. I have a minor book.
    b. Jolie has a minor dress.
    c. That is a minor soccer ball.
    d. I had a minor problem with my homework.

Name _____

Day 5 important • importance • main • minor

Fill in the bubble next to the correct answer.

1. An *important* thing to do when riding in a car is _____.

- Ⓐ sing
- Ⓑ fasten your seat belt
- Ⓒ take a snack
- Ⓓ look out the window

2. Which sentence uses *importance* correctly?

- Ⓕ The importance of apples is red.
- Ⓖ There is not a great importance of money.
- Ⓗ It is importance to get exercise.
- Ⓙ I know the importance of doing my homework.

3. What is the *main* reason to play soccer?

- Ⓐ to kick hard
- Ⓑ to wear shorts
- Ⓒ to drink water
- Ⓓ to have fun

4. Which one is a *minor* part of sending a letter?

- Ⓕ writing the letter
- Ⓖ addressing the envelope
- Ⓗ decorating the paper
- Ⓙ putting a stamp on the front of the envelope

Writing Think of your favorite room in your home. What is the *main* part of the room? What is a *minor* part? Use the words *main* and *minor* in your writing.

_____

_____

_____

© Evan-Moor Corporation • EMC 2758 • Daily Academic Vocabulary **WEEK 2** 17

Daily Academic Vocabulary

WEEK 3

common • in common
uncommon • special

Use the reproducible definitions on page 162 and the suggestions on page 6 to introduce the words for each day.

DAY 1

common
(adj.) Happening often. *The school bus is a **common** way to get to school.*

Say these sentences aloud: *Cars parked on the street, houses, and apartment buildings are **common** sights. We see them all the time.* Ask: *What **common** things happen in our classroom?* Then conduct the first activity for Day 1 on page 19. Have students complete the Day 1 activities on their own, in pairs, or in a group.

DAY 2

common
(adj.) Shared by two or more things or people; shared by each and all. *My brother and I have a **common** interest in swimming.*

in common
(phrase) Shared by two or more things or people; shared by each and all. *My new neighbor and I have many things **in common**.*

Have students point to and name objects in the room that are **common** and shared by all. (e.g., globe; books; computer) Next, display a textbook and a storybook. Ask: *What **common** features do these two things share?* (Both are books with words.) Then explain that the word **common** is often used in the phrase **in common**. Say as an example: *One thing I have **in common** with you is this school.* Ask: *What do you have **in common** with each other?* Then have students choose two items from their desk and tell what they have **in common**. (e.g., pen and pencil are both used for writing) Conduct the first activity for Day 2 on page 19. Have students complete the Day 2 activities on their own, in pairs, or as a group.

DAY 3

uncommon
(adj.) Not happening often. *It is **uncommon** to see a purple car.*

Explain to students that the prefix "un-" means "not." So, **uncommon** means "not common." Ask: *What would be **uncommon** to see on your street or in your neighborhood?* (e.g., a circus parade; a rock star) Be sure they include happenings, as well as sights, that are **uncommon**, but not impossible. Conduct the first activity for Day 3 on page 20. Have students complete the Day 3 activities on their own, in pairs, or as a group.

DAY 4

special
(adj.) Different from other things or people. *I gave my mother the **special** scarf I made.*

Display an object that has meaning to you, such as a pen, a piece of jewelry, or a book, and explain why that object is **special** to you. Then ask: *What **special** thing do you own or would you like to own?* After answers, ask: *What makes it **special**?* Conduct the first activity for Day 4 on page 20. Then have students complete the Day 4 activities on their own, in pairs, or as a group.

DAY 5

Have students complete page 21. Call on students to read aloud their answers to the writing activity.

Name_____

Daily Academic Vocabulary

Day 1 common

1. How would you complete this sentence? Say it aloud.

   _____ is a common happening during the school day.

2. What is a *common* activity on the playground?
   Circle your answers.

   a. swinging on swings
   b. taking tests
   c. sliding down slides
   d. swimming underwater

3. What is a *common* thing that students wear in the classroom?
   Circle your answer.

   a. helmets   c. bathing suits
   b. shirts   d. life jackets

Day 2 common • in common

1. How would you complete these sentences? Say them aloud.

   The classrooms in our school share a common _____.

   One thing I have in common with my best friend is _____.

2. What *common* interests do parents and teachers share?
   Circle your answers.

   a. children   c. learning
   b. horses   d. ice-skating

3. What do a train and a bicycle have *in common*?
   Circle your answer.

   a. They both have four wheels.
   b. They are both blue.
   c. They both have engines.
   d. They are both used to get to places.

© Evan-Moor Corporation • EMC 2758 • Daily Academic Vocabulary   WEEK 3   19

Name_____

Daily Academic Vocabulary

Day 3 uncommon

1. How would you complete this sentence? Say it aloud.

   It is uncommon for me to eat _____.

2. What is an *uncommon* thing to see in a city?
   Circle your answer.

   a. street signs   c. cars and trucks
   b. a cow   d. traffic lights

3. Which sentence uses the word *uncommon* correctly?
   Circle your answer.

   a. The desert is uncommon hot.
   b. An uncommon sight in school is books.
   c. Snow is uncommon in Florida.
   d. Can you uncommon the knot in my laces?

Day 4 special

1. How would you complete this sentence? Say it aloud.

   I think special gifts are things that _____.

2. What day is *special* for most people?
   Circle your answer.

   a. Monday   c. their birthday
   b. Tuesday   d. a cloudy day

3. Who would be a *special* visitor to your school?
   Circle your answer.

   a. a teacher
   b. a firefighter
   c. a school principal
   d. a school nurse

20 WEEK 3   Daily Academic Vocabulary • EMC 2758 • © Evan-Moor Corporation

Name_____

Day 5 | common • in common
uncommon • special

Fill in the bubble next to the correct answer.

1. Yellow is a *common* color for _____.
   - Ⓐ pencils
   - Ⓑ books
   - Ⓒ floors
   - Ⓓ trees

2. What do soccer and kickball have *in common*?
   - Ⓕ goalies
   - Ⓖ bases
   - Ⓗ teams
   - Ⓙ pitchers

3. What is an *uncommon* sight in the sky?
   - Ⓐ the sun
   - Ⓑ the space shuttle
   - Ⓒ clouds
   - Ⓓ birds

4. A *special* thing you could do for a friend on his or her birthday is _____.
   - Ⓕ take a nap
   - Ⓖ make a card
   - Ⓗ ride a bike
   - Ⓙ read a book

Writing Describe the *common* and *uncommon* things that happen in your home. Use the words *common* and *uncommon* in your writing.

_____

_____

_____

Daily Academic Vocabulary

WEEK 4

equal • alike • unlike

Use the reproducible definitions on page 163 and the suggestions on page 6 to introduce the words for each day.

DAY 1

equal
(adj.) The same in size, value, or amount. *Four quarters and one dollar are **equal** amounts.*

Fill three glasses with colored water, two with the same amount. Line them up on a desk or table so students can see them. Ask: *Which of these glasses have the same amount of water?* Say: *Those glasses have **equal** amounts of water. They have the same amount.* Then name two pairs of objects (e.g., classroom chairs; a bicycle and a car) and ask if they are **equal** in size, value, or amount. Finally, conduct the first activity for Day 1 on page 23. Then have students complete the Day 1 activities on their own, in pairs, or as a group.

DAY 2

equal
(verb) To be the same as, or equal to, something else. *Two dimes and a nickel **equal** a quarter.*

Remind students that they know this word from math. Ask: *What does two plus two **equal**?* Next, have two students stand in front of the class. Give each of them two books. Ask: *Does the number of books (student's name) holds **equal** the number of books (student's name) holds?* (Yes.) *Why?* (They are holding the same number of books.) Then conduct the first activity for Day 2 on page 23. Have students complete the Day 2 activities on their own, in pairs, or as a group.

DAY 3

alike
(adj.) Looking or acting the same way. *These pictures are **alike** because they are both drawings of a daisy.*

Choose two objects in the room that have similarities. Ask: *How are these things **alike**?* Then have students take turns choosing two objects in the room and telling how they are **alike**. Finally, conduct the first activity for Day 3 on page 24. Then have students complete the Day 3 activities on their own, in pairs, or as a group.

DAY 4

unlike
(prep.) Different. *This rock is **unlike** the others because it is shiny.*

Choose five objects in the room, four of which are similar, or go together, in some way. Line them up on a table or desk. Ask: *Which of these things is different from, or **unlike**, the others? How is it **unlike** the others?* Next, choose two familiar animals. (e.g., elephant and parrot; dog and goldfish) Ask: *How is a ___ **unlike** a ___?* Then conduct the first activity for Day 4 on page 24. Have students complete the Day 4 activities on their own, in pairs, or as a group.

DAY 5

Have students complete page 25. Call on students to read aloud their answers to the writing activity.

Name_____

Day 1 equal

1. How would you complete this sentence? Say it aloud.

   A book is not equal in size to a __table__.

2. Which of these are *equal* amounts? Circle your answer.

   a. 1 tablespoon of flour and 1 teaspoon of sugar
   b. 1 teaspoon of water and 1 cup of sugar
   c. 1 cup of flour and 1 cup of milk
   d. 1 tablespoon of flour and 1 teaspoon of milk

3. Which sentence means that everyone has an *equal* amount of time to do something? Circle your answer.

   a. Everyone has a different amount of time.
   b. Everyone has close to the same amount of time.
   c. Everyone has several amounts of time.
   d. Everyone has the same amount of time.

Day 2 equal

1. How would you complete this sentence? Say it aloud.

   One dollar equals _____.

2. Which amount of water *equals* the amount in the first glass? Circle your answer.

   a.   **b.**   c.

3. Which ones do <u>not</u> *equal* 10? Circle your answers.

   a. 5 + 5   **b.** 2 + 9   **c.** 2 + 4   d. 9 + 1

Name _____

Day 3 alike   4/22

1. How would you complete this sentence? Say it aloud.

   My teacher and I are alike because _____.

2. Which of these are *alike*? Circle your answers.

   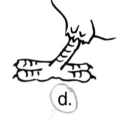

   a.   b.   c.   d.

   (a and d circled)

3. Which sentence uses the word *alike* correctly? Circle your answer.

   a. The girls are in the same alike grade.
   b. The school alike the other school.
   c. The students' jackets are alike.
   d. I think alike the teacher.

Day 4 unlike

1. How would you complete this sentence? Say it aloud.

   Art is unlike math because its different.

2. Which number is *unlike* the others? Circle your answer.

   a. 2   c. 13
   b. 4   d. 6

3. Which word means the same as *unlike*? Circle your answer.

   a. same   c. different
   b. alike   d. strange

24 WEEK 4

Name_____

Day 5 equal • alike • unlike

Fill in the bubble next to the correct answer.

1. We all have an *equal* chance to finish the test because we _____.
   - Ⓐ start at the same time
   - Ⓑ start at different times
   - Ⓒ take turns
   - Ⓓ work slowly

2. Which sentence uses the word *equal* correctly?
   - Ⓕ I equals Ava in the race.
   - Ⓖ Noah's time equals Sarah's time.
   - Ⓗ How many equals are the books?
   - Ⓙ 10 equals 2.

3. How are a circle and a square *alike*?
   - Ⓐ They are both round.
   - Ⓑ They both have four sides.
   - Ⓒ They are both shapes.
   - Ⓓ They are both triangles.

4. Which word is *unlike* the others?
   - Ⓕ pencil
   - Ⓖ pen
   - Ⓗ marker
   - Ⓙ paper

Writing Think about two friends. How are they *alike*? How are they different? Use the words *alike* and *unlike* in your writing.

Shara and shophie are diffrent Sharg has long hair but shophie dousent.

Daily Academic Vocabulary

WEEK 5

combine • combination
connect • connection

Use the reproducible definitions on page 164 and the suggestions on page 6 to introduce the words for each day.

DAY 1

combine
(verb) To bring together or join together into a whole. *When you **combine** lemons, sugar, and water, you make lemonade.*

Ask: *What would you **combine** to make a fruit salad?* Say: *When we **combine** all of these separate fruits, we bring them together to make a fruit salad. What else can you **combine**?* (e.g., colors; clothes; words) Have students respond by saying, *"I can **combine** ___ to make ___."* Then conduct the first activity for Day 1 on page 27. Have students complete the Day 1 activities on their own, in pairs, or as a group.

DAY 2

combination
(noun) Things that have come together or have been brought together. *The **combination** of peanut butter and jelly makes a delicious sandwich!*

Say: *When you combine things, it makes a **combination**.* Ask: *What **combination** of toppings do you like on your pizza? What **combination** makes your favorite snack?* Then ask: *Can you think of other **combinations** that aren't food, such as papier-mâché?* (paste and newspaper) Ask students why their responses are **combinations**. Then conduct the first activity for Day 2 on page 27. Have students complete the Day 2 activities on their own, in pairs, or as a group.

DAY 3

connect
(verb) To join together or link. *The sidewalks **connect** the two buildings of our school.*

Draw two dots on the board. Ask: *What's the best way to **connect** these dots?* Draw a line between the dots. Say: *When two things **connect**, they are brought together or linked in some way. For example, two puzzle pieces **connect**.* Ask: *What things in this room **connect** to each other?* Brainstorm a list and write it on the board. Then conduct the first activity for Day 3 on page 28. Have students complete the Day 3 activities on their own, in pairs, or as a group.

DAY 4

connection
(noun) A link or relationship between two things. *There is a **connection** between eating healthy food and feeling good.*

Say: *Things that are connected have a **connection**. A **connection** can be a link or relationship. For instance, there is a **connection** between heavy traffic and pollution. Because of heavy traffic, we get pollution.* Brainstorm other such **connections**, both positive and negative, and write them on the board. Then conduct the first activity for Day 4 on page 28. Have students complete the Day 4 activities on their own, in pairs, or as a group.

DAY 5

Have students complete page 29. Call on students to read aloud their answers to the writing activity.

Name_____

Day 1 combine

1. How would you complete this sentence? Say it aloud.

    I could combine __ham__ and __cheese__ to make a sandwich.

2. What could you *combine* with milk to make something that tastes good? Circle your answer.

    a. pickles
    b. salt
    c. paper
    (d.) chocolate

3. Which sentence uses the word *combine* correctly? Circle your answer.

    a. Tina uses a combine of pencils and colored markers to draw.
    (b.) She will combine flour and water to make paste.
    c. Jorge will combine about his art project with his teacher.
    d. He can combine this project on his own.

Day 2 combination

1. How would you complete this sentence? Say it aloud.

    My favorite soup is a combination of __Chilli__ and __cheese__.

2. Which of the following is a *combination*? Circle your answer.

    a. a bright red bicycle
    (b.) a bubble mixture made from dishwashing soap and water
    c. fresh water in a river
    d. a pair of new pants

3. Which one best completes this sentence? Circle your answer.

    A combination is always _____.

    a. made with water
    b. made of something soft
    (c.) made up of more than one thing
    d. made up of four sides

I love this combination of flavors!

Name _____

Day 3 connect

1. How would you complete this sentence? Say it aloud.

    You have to connect _____ to _____ to make it work.

2. What does a leash *connect*? Circle your answer.

    a. a dog and its owner
    b. a fence
    c. a dog
    d. an owner

3. Which one best completes the sentence? Circle your answer.

    You can use glue to connect _____.

    a. a hallway
    b. two pieces of something
    c. more glue
    d. water

Day 4 connection

1. How would you complete this sentence? Say it aloud.

    There is a connection between doing my homework and _____.

2. Which ones are examples of a *connection*? Circle your answers.

    a. the sun and snow
    b. the hot sun and a sunburn
    c. two dogs and two cats
    d. doing homework and getting a good grade

3. Which sentence uses *connection* correctly? Circle your answer.

    a. The highway will connection one city to another.
    b. There is a connection between running fast and being out of breath.
    c. There is a connection between paper and water.
    d. The connection of blue and red makes purple.

28   **WEEK 5**   Daily Academic Vocabulary • EMC 2758 • © Evan-Moor Corporation

Name_____

Day 5 | combine • combination
connect • connection

Fill in the bubble next to the correct answer.

1. Which one means the same thing as *combine*?
- Ⓐ bring together
- Ⓑ pull apart
- Ⓒ open wide
- Ⓓ shut tight

2. Which sentence uses *combination* correctly?
- Ⓕ A hat is a combination of clothes.
- Ⓖ A storm is a combination of rain.
- Ⓗ A zoo is a combination of one kind of animal.
- Ⓙ A song is a combination of words and music.

3. Which one would be a way to *connect* two cities?
- Ⓐ build a road
- Ⓑ cut down trees
- Ⓒ buy a plane ticket
- Ⓓ rent a car

4. Which one is a *connection*?
- Ⓕ one person walking to the park
- Ⓖ eating lunch and eating dinner
- Ⓗ taking a bath and smelling good
- Ⓙ wearing different clothes than your friend

Writing   Describe a *combination* that makes a good story. What do you think a good story needs? Use the word *combination* in your writing.

_____

_____

_____

Daily Academic Vocabulary

WEEK 6: correct • correction

Use the reproducible definitions on page 165 and the suggestions on page 6 to introduce the words for each day.

DAY 1

correct
(verb) To fix mistakes in something or make it right. *Proofread your paper and **correct** any spelling mistakes.*

Write a short sentence on the board and leave out the period. Say: *This sentence has a mistake. I will **correct** it.* Add the period. Next, write simple math problems on the board with incorrect answers. Have volunteers take turns **correcting** the answers, saying, "This is how to **correct** the mistake." Then conduct the first activity for Day 1 on page 31. Have students complete the Day 1 activities on their own, in pairs, or as a group.

DAY 2

correct
(adj.) Having no mistakes. *That answer is **correct**.*

Write these words on the board: "soon," "now," "first," "then." Say: *The spelling is **correct** for each of these words.* Then write "says" and "sez" on the board. Ask: *Which word has the **correct** spelling?* Then ask: *What does **correct** mean when the spelling of a word is **correct**? What does it mean if the answer on a test is **correct**? If a math problem is **correct**?* Then conduct the first activity for Day 2 on page 31. Have students complete the Day 2 activities on their own, in pairs, or as a group.

DAY 3

correct
(verb) To mark errors or point out mistakes in something. *Our teacher will **correct** our spelling papers and give us a grade.*

Write several simple math problems on the board, half incorrect. Ask: *Will you help me **correct** these problems?* Ask students to come to the board and mark the incorrect problems with an *X*. Say: *You just **corrected** these problems. You did not fix or change the mistakes, but you pointed out which problems were incorrect.* Ask: *What are other examples of someone **correcting** something?* (pointing out a wrong answer or mistake; **correcting** a mispronunciation) Then conduct the first activity for Day 3 on page 32. Have students complete the Day 3 activities on their own, in pairs, or as a group.

DAY 4

correction
(noun) Something put in the place of something wrong. *I misspelled the word, so I erased it and made a **correction**.*

Write on the board: 7 + 3 = 11. Then say: *This answer is wrong. I'll make a **correction**.* Erase *11* and write *10*. Write other incorrect problems and have students make the **corrections**. Have them identify the **corrections** they made. Ask: *What other **corrections** do you make at school?* (spelling words; grammar) Then conduct the first activity for Day 4 on page 32. Have students complete the Day 4 activities on their own, in pairs, or as a group.

DAY 5

Have students complete page 33. Call on students to read aloud their answers to the writing activity.

Name _____

Day 1 correct

1. How would you complete this sentence? Say it aloud.

   One kind of mistake that is easy for me to correct is _____.

2. Which one means the opposite of *correct*? Circle your answer.

   a. fix
   b. change
   c. make something right
   d. make something wrong

3. In which sentence can *correct* replace the underlined word? Circle your answer.

   a. Rob always <u>combs</u> his hair after he washes it.
   b. Can he <u>change</u> one dollar for ten dimes?
   c. Lita will <u>change</u> the spelling of "kee" to make it "key."
   d. Can she <u>explain</u> how day turns to night?

Day 2 correct

1. How would you complete this sentence? Say it aloud.

   I always get the correct answers when _____.

2. Which sentence correctly uses the word *correct*? Circle your answer.

   a. Yes, that is the correct answer.
   b. I'm going to make a correct in my spelling.
   c. That book report is correct and full of mistakes.
   d. A correct mistake needs to be fixed.

3. Which word means the same thing as *correct*?

   a. wrong   c. colorful
   b. important d. right

Name_____

Day 3   correct

1. How would you complete this sentence? Say it aloud.

My teacher uses a _____ to correct our papers.

2. Which sentence uses *correct* in the right way? Circle your answer.

    a. Our teacher washes the chalkboard to correct it.
    b. My dad corrects the different birds in the park.
    c. I correct the light by walking when it is green.
    d. Ms. Lowe uses a check mark to correct math papers.

3. How would your teacher *correct* a spelling test mistake? Circle your answer.

    a. Write a different answer.   c. Mark the error.
    b. Leave it the way it is.   d. Erase it and write it the wrong way.

Day 4   correction

1. How would you complete this sentence? Say it aloud.

One correction I often need to make in my writing is _____.

2. Which one describes a *correction*? Circle your answer.

    a. counting the mistakes on a test
    b. fixing something that isn't right
    c. finding a mistake
    d. not making a mistake

3. Which statements are true about *corrections*? Circle your answers.

    a. You make corrections after you make mistakes.
    b. You make corrections when there are no mistakes.
    c. Corrections help you make more mistakes.
    d. Corrections change wrong answers to right answers.

Name_____

Daily Academic Vocabulary

Day 5 correct • correction

Fill in the bubble next to the correct answer.

1. How would you *correct* this sentence?

The frog jumped into the watr.

Ⓐ Make the "f" in "frog" a capital letter.
Ⓑ Fix the spelling of "water."
Ⓒ Change the period to a question mark.
Ⓓ Do not change anything.

2. Which statement is *correct*?

Ⓕ Holidays are always in August.
Ⓖ All holidays celebrate spring.
Ⓗ The first holiday took place this year.
Ⓙ One holiday celebrates the new year.

3. What does your teacher do when he or she *corrects* students' work?

Ⓐ Your teacher changes your work.
Ⓑ Your teacher points out your mistakes.
Ⓒ Your teacher ignores your mistakes.
Ⓓ Your teacher makes the same mistakes you have made.

4. A *correction* makes something that was wrong into something that is _____.

Ⓕ right
Ⓖ wrong
Ⓗ the same
Ⓙ equal

Writing Think about a time when you *corrected* something. Write about what you learned by making that *correction*. Use *correct* or *correction* in your writing.

_____

_____

_____

© Evan-Moor Corporation • EMC 2758 • Daily Academic Vocabulary   **WEEK 6**   33

Daily Academic Vocabulary

WEEK 7

explain • example

Use the reproducible definitions on page 166 and the suggestions on page 6 to introduce the words for each day.

DAY 1

explain
(verb) To tell about something in a way that is easy to understand. *The teacher will **explain** how to do the science experiment.*

Ask: *How do you make a peanut butter sandwich?* Write the steps on the board. Say: *This recipe **explains** how to make a peanut butter sandwich.* Then ask: *What other things can you **explain** how to do?* Then conduct the first activity for Day 1 on page 35. Have students complete the Day 1 activities on their own, in pairs, or as a group.

DAY 2

explain
(verb) To give a reason why. *The boy should **explain** why he was late to school.*

Say: *Think about a favorite book.* Ask: *What do you like about it? Who would like to **explain** the reason why that book is your favorite?* Call on several students. Then ask: *When the students **explained** their choices, did you learn the reasons why they feel that way?* Say: ***Explain** can also mean to tell the reason why something happened.* Ask: *Have your parents or an adult at school ever asked you to give a reason why you did something? They wanted you to **explain** your actions.* Then conduct the first activity for Day 2 on page 35. Have students complete the Day 2 activities on their own, in pairs, or as a group.

DAY 3

example
(noun) Something that is picked out to show what other things of its type or group are like. *A lemon is an **example** of something that is sour.*

Hold up or display different kinds of books, such as a book on a science topic, a biography, a fairy tale, and a textbook. Then identify them. For **example**, say: *This is an **example** of a biography, a story of a person's life.* Ask questions, such as: *Which book is an **example** of (a fairy tale)?* until all the books have been identified. Then conduct the first activity for Day 3 on page 36. Have students complete the Day 3 activities on their own, in pairs, or as a group.

DAY 4

example
(noun) A problem that is worked out in order to show how to answer other problems of this type. *The **example** helped me figure out how to solve the math problem.*

Have students turn to a page in their math textbook with an **example** on it and say: *Find the **example** on page ___. What does it show you how to do?* Have students look through the book and identify other **examples**. Encourage them to use the word **example**. Then conduct the first activity for Day 4 on page 36. Have students complete the Day 4 activities on their own, in pairs, or as a group.

DAY 5

Have students complete page 37. Call on students to read aloud their answers to the writing activity.

Name_____

Daily Academic Vocabulary

Day 1 explain

1. How would you complete this sentence? Say it aloud.

    I can explain how to _____.

2. Which sentence uses *explain* correctly? Circle your answer.

    a. Take a flashlight when you explain the cave.
    b. I explain him to be here at noon.
    c. Sam will explain how he makes pancakes.
    d. His explain of how to play football was hard to understand.

3. *Explain* how to make chocolate milk.

    _____

    _____

    _____

Day 2 explain

1. How would you complete this sentence? Say it aloud.

    I can explain why I _____.

2. Tricia comes home covered in mud. What would her parents want her to *explain*? Circle your answer.

    a. why her clothes are dirty   c. what is on television
    b. what movie she saw   d. how hot it is outside

3. *Explain* why you should get an allowance.

    _____

    _____

    _____

Name_____

Day 3 example

1. How would you complete this sentence? Say it aloud.

   One example of a dessert is _____.

2. Which one is an *example* of where a person might live? Circle your answer.

         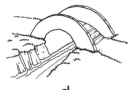

   a.   b.   c.   d.

3. Which sentence uses *example* correctly? Circle your answer.

   a. A dog is an example of a common pet.
   b. An example of nuts and raisins are used to make a snack.
   c. One example of milk equals two pints.
   d. Can you example that problem?

Day 4 example

1. How would you complete this sentence? Say it aloud.

   Examples help me to _____.

2. Which one is an *example* that shows how to add? Circle your answer.

   a.

   b.

   c.

   d.

3. What is an *example* of a fairy tale?

   _____

Name_____

Day 5 explain • example

Fill in the bubble next to the correct answer.

1. Which sentence would *explain* how to get somewhere?
   - Ⓐ Going new places is exciting.
   - Ⓑ Turn right and then walk ten feet.
   - Ⓒ The market is a place where you can buy food.
   - Ⓓ Walking is good exercise.

2. Which sentence would *explain* why school is closed?
   - Ⓕ The teacher is there.
   - Ⓖ The children are in their seats.
   - Ⓗ It is Saturday.
   - Ⓙ It is the first day of school.

3. Which one is an *example* of rhyming words?
   - Ⓐ hot, hat
   - Ⓑ hot, pot
   - Ⓒ splash, splat
   - Ⓓ hat, has

4. How can an *example* help you with a math problem?
   - Ⓕ It can do your work for you.
   - Ⓖ It can show you what you are supposed to do.
   - Ⓗ It can show you a spelling mistake.
   - Ⓙ It can add and subtract.

Writing What are two *examples* of ways you can travel to school? *Explain* why each way is a good way. Use the word *example* in your answer.

_____

_____

_____

Daily Academic Vocabulary

agree • agreement • disagree

Use the reproducible definitions on page 167 and the suggestions on page 6 to introduce the words for each day.

DAY 1

agree
(verb) To think the same way about something. *My sister and I agree that summer is the best season.*

Say: *I thought yesterday was cooler (warmer) than today. How many of you agree?* Make a number of other statements, asking students to raise their hands if they **agree**. (e.g., *The best book is…*) Then invite volunteers to make their own statements, asking classmates to raise their hands if they **agree**. Conduct the first activity for Day 1 on page 39. Then have students complete the Day 1 activities on their own, in pairs, or as a group.

DAY 2

agree
(verb) To say yes to something. *We agree to help our father clean the house.*

Say: *Raise your hand if you agree with each question I will ask. How many of you agree to go outside and play today? How many of you agree to do your homework tonight?* Have volunteers answer each question, using the word **agree**. For example, "I **agree** to go outside and play." Then conduct the first activity for Day 2 on page 39. Have students complete the Day 2 activities on their own, in pairs, or as a group.

DAY 3

agreement
(noun) An understanding between two or more persons or groups. *The club members made an agreement to meet once a week.*

Say: *An agreement is like a promise to do something. Your school day and home lives are made up of many agreements. For example, you agree to behave in class.* Ask: *What other agreements do we make at school?* (to do our homework; to be quiet at certain times; to raise our hands) Ask: *What other agreements do you make? Why are agreements important?* Encourage students to use the word **agreement** in their responses. Then conduct the first activity for Day 3 on page 40. Have students complete the Day 3 activities on their own, in pairs, or as a group.

DAY 4

disagree
(verb) To have a different feeling or belief from someone else. *My friend and I disagree about who is the best singer in our class.*

Say: *Agree and disagree are opposites. If "agree" means to think the same way as someone, what does disagree mean?* Say: *I think soccer is boring. How many agree? How many disagree?* Invite students to make up their own statements, asking other students to raise their hands to agree or **disagree**. Then conduct the first activity for Day 4 on page 40. Have students complete the Day 4 activities on their own, in pairs, or as a group.

DAY 5

Have students complete page 41. Call on students to read aloud their answers to the writing activity.

38   Daily Academic Vocabulary • EMC 2758 • © Evan-Moor Corporation

Name _____

Daily Academic Vocabulary

Day 1 — agree

1. **How would you complete this sentence? Say it aloud.**

    I agree with my teacher that _____.

2. **Which one would most people *agree* with? Circle your answer.**

    a. All books are big and heavy.
    b. Math is the easiest subject.
    c. School is a good place to learn.
    d. Books are the only way to learn new things.

3. **Which sentence uses *agree* correctly? Circle your answer.**

    a. Ben agrees his dad to go fishing.
    b. I agree with Ben's house at 7 a.m.
    c. Our agree is to try to catch lots of fish.
    d. Ben and I agree that fishing is fun.

Day 2 — agree

1. **How would you complete this sentence? Say it aloud.**

    At home, I always agree to _____.

2. **Kayla's parents say that she doesn't get enough sleep. What might they ask her to *agree* to do if tomorrow is a school day? Circle your answer.**

    a. wash her clothes   c. eat a big dinner
    b. watch television   d. go to bed early

3. **What is something you would *agree* to do?**

    I would agree to _____

    _____

    _____

© Evan-Moor Corporation • EMC 2758 • Daily Academic Vocabulary   WEEK 8   39

Name _____

Day 3 agreement

1. How would you complete this sentence? Say it aloud.

   The members of my family have an agreement to _____.

2. Which one is an example of an *agreement*? Circle your answer.

   a. Two children look inside a toy store.
   b. A girl rides a bike.
   c. A brother and sister fight over toys.
   d. A brother and sister promise not to fight over toys.

3. Which sentence does not use *agreement* correctly? Circle your answer.

   a. The teachers came to an agreement on the date for the school play.
   b. The teachers and students agreement on different songs.
   c. The students are in agreement to clean up after lunch.
   d. The teachers and students made an agreement to go on a field trip.

Day 4 disagree

1. How would you complete this sentence? Say it aloud.

   I disagree with _____ about _____.

2. Which one would most people *disagree* with? Circle your answer.

   a. Exercise helps keep us strong.
   b. An apple is a better snack than a candy bar.
   c. Children need only one hour of sleep each night.
   d. Children need at least eight hours of sleep each night.

3. Which sentence uses *disagree* correctly? Circle your answer.

   a. My father and I disagree about which ice cream is the best.
   b. My teacher and I are in disagree about homework.
   c. My friend and I disagree because we both think that apples are the best.
   d. My mom disagrees me when she sends me to my room.

Name_____

Day 5 agree • agreement • disagree

Daily Academic Vocabulary

Fill in the bubble next to the correct answer.

1. Which statement would most people *agree* with?
    - Ⓐ It is important to have a lot of chairs.
    - Ⓑ It is important to collect paper clips.
    - Ⓒ It is important to yell at everyone.
    - Ⓓ It is important to be kind to other people.

2. Which sentence uses *agree* correctly?
    - Ⓕ I agree to help clean up after the party.
    - Ⓖ I agree in the morning after I brush my teeth.
    - Ⓗ I will be in agree at 9:00.
    - Ⓙ Can I agree over that later?

3. An *agreement* is made when _____.
    - Ⓐ one person tells you what to do
    - Ⓑ two or more people do different things
    - Ⓒ two or more people reach an understanding
    - Ⓓ everyone thinks something different

4. What is the opposite of *disagree*?
    - Ⓕ example
    - Ⓖ explain
    - Ⓗ agree
    - Ⓙ agreement

Writing Think of someone in your family. Write about what you *agree* on. Then write what you *disagree* on. Use *agree* and *disagree* in your writing.

_____

_____

_____

CUMULATIVE REVIEW
WORDS FROM WEEKS 1–8

agree
agreement
alike
combination
combine
common
connect
connection
correct
correction
disagree
equal
example
explain
fact
importance
important
in common
main
minor
opinion
special
test
uncommon
unlike

Days 1–4
Each day's activity is a cloze paragraph that students complete with words or forms of words that they have learned in weeks 1–8. Before students begin, pronounce each word in the box on the student page, have students repeat each word, and then review each word's meaning(s). **Other ways to review the words:**

- Start a sentence containing one of the words and have students finish the sentence orally. For example:

    *One of the most **common** animals in our neighborhood is…*
    *I think that every day it is very **important** to…*

- Provide students with a definition and ask them to supply the word that fits it.
- Ask questions that require students to know the meaning of each word. For example:

    *What is one **example** of an animal that lives in the ocean?*
    *How are a river and a lake **alike**?*

- Have students use each word in a sentence.

Day 5
Start by reviewing the words in the crossword activity for Day 5. Write the words on the board and have students repeat them after you. Provide a sentence for one of the words. Ask students to think of their own sentence and share it with a partner. Call on several students to share their sentences. Follow the same procedure for the remaining words. Then have students complete the crossword activity.

Extension Ideas
Use any of the following activities to help integrate the vocabulary words into other content areas:

- Have students experiment with mixing colors. Ask them to tell what colors you can **combine** to create orange, purple, and green. Then ask them to share their **opinions** about favorite colors.
- Ask students to write sentences to describe the **main** things they do at school each day. Then have students describe two **minor** things they do each day. Have students work in pairs to **correct** their work.
- Have students pick two animals to study. They should create a poster that illustrates how their pair of animals is **alike** and **unlike**.
- Hold a Geography Quest. Name **examples** of countries, states, cities, mountains, lakes, rivers, and deserts to find on a simple map. Ask students to **explain** how they located that place.

Name _____

Daily Academic Vocabulary

| agreement | connection | example | important |
| combine | correct | facts | in common |

Day 1

Fill in the blanks with words from the word box.

Did you know that there is a __connection__ between birds and dinosaurs? Today's birds have things __in common__ with prehistoric dinosaurs. For __example__, scientists have found dinosaur bones that have hollow spots in them like bird bones. This is an __important__ discovery.

Day 2

Fill in the blanks with words from the word box.

Amy's team was working on a report using the Internet. First, they reached an __agreement__ about what to study. They decided to look for __facts__ about gray whales. They visited four different Web sites. When they wrote their report, they tried to __combine__ ideas from the sites they visited. After they wrote the report, they read it again to __correct__ any mistakes.

WEEK 9

Name_____

Daily Academic Vocabulary

| agree | corrections | main | opinion |
| combination | explain | minor | uncommon |

Day 3

Fill in the blanks with words from the word box.

A scientist came to our class to __explain__ how diamonds form. The __main__ idea was that diamonds are made of something called carbon. Heat and high pressure deep in the Earth can cause the carbon to turn into diamonds. He also shared his __corrections__ that the most beautiful jewelry is made from diamonds. Because diamonds are expensive, it is __uncommon__ for people to own a lot of them.

Day 4

Fill in the blanks with words from the word box.

I asked my sister to read my short story. She said it was an interesting __combination__ of scary and funny parts. She also found some __main__ mistakes. For example, I spelled one word incorrectly. Her __opinion__ helped me fix my story. She and I both __agree__ that the story is much better now.

Name _____

Day 5

Crossword Challenge

For each clue, write one of the words from the word box to complete the puzzle.

alike   connect   equals   special   unlike
common   disagree   importance   test

Down
1. not the same
3. 4 plus 7 ___ 11
5. something that is ___ is different from other things
6. a big quiz

Across
2. to join together
4. happening often
7. if something has value or meaning, it has ___
8. looking the same
9. to have a different opinion from someone else

© Evan-Moor Corporation • EMC 2758 • Daily Academic Vocabulary   **WEEK 9**   45

Daily Academic Vocabulary

WEEK 10: list • item • group

Use the reproducible definitions on page 168 and the suggestions on page 6 to introduce the words for each day.

DAY 1

list
(verb) To say or write down things that fit in a group. *The teacher will **list** the names of students in our class.*

(noun) A set of things that are written down. *Mom made a **list** of clothes to buy for school.*

Say: *I'm going to **list** some of the things I have in my desk drawer.* Write the items on the board. While you are doing so, say: *When I use the word **list** in this way, it shows action. It tells what I do.* Then circle the group of items and say: *This is the **list** I made. It is a set of things.* Next, call on several students to orally **list** the things in their desks. Write the items on the board as students say them. Say: *I **listed** the things that were named. This is the **list** of items that are in the desks.* Then conduct the first activity for Day 1 on page 47. Have students complete the Day 1 activities on their own, in pairs, or as a group.

DAY 2

item
(noun) One of a number of things. *We made a list of each **item** we needed at the store.*

Tell students that you want to make a list of **items** to get at the store to make sandwiches. Ask: *What **items** should I put on my list?* As students volunteer an **item**, write it in a list on the board. Then ask: *What **items** would we need to paint a picture?* Finally, conduct the first activity for Day 2 on page 47. Have students complete the Day 2 activities on their own, in pairs, or as a group.

DAY 3

group
(noun) A number of persons or things that go together or are put together. *Ms. Wong showed the **group** of new students around the school.*

Display a collection of pencils and say: *This is a **group** of pencils. You are a **group** of students.* Ask: *What other **groups** could you make with the people and items that are in this room? For example, I could make a **group** of all the girls.* Allow individuals to respond by completing the sentence, "I could make a **group** of ___." Then conduct the first activity for Day 3 on page 48. Have students complete the Day 3 activities on their own, in pairs, or as a group.

DAY 4

group
(verb) To put persons or things together in a group. *The principal will **group** the students by grade.*

Say: *The word **group** can also show action. Let's **group** you by clothing. All students who are wearing blue stand up. Everyone who is wearing red stand up. I just **grouped** you by the color of your clothing.* After students sit down, ask: *What are some other ways we could **group** people?* (e.g., height; age; favorite sport) Then conduct the first activity for Day 4 on page 48. Have students complete the Day 4 activities on their own, in pairs, or as a group.

DAY 5

Have students complete page 49. Call on students to read aloud their answers to the writing activity.

Name_____

Day 1 list

1. How would you complete this sentence? Say it aloud.

    My list of favorite foods would be _____.

2. What does it mean to *list* the homework that is due tomorrow? Circle your answer.

    a. to buy pencils and paper
    b. to finish your homework
    c. to write a letter
    d. to write down what you have to do

3. Which one does not belong on a *list* of chores? Circle your answer.

    a. clean your room
    b. put your dirty clothes in the hamper
    c. milk, eggs, and bread
    d. dry the dishes

Day 2 item

1. How would you complete this sentence? Say it aloud.

    Items that I take to school every day are _____.

2. Which ones are *items* that you might find in a closet? Circle your answers.

    a. a hat   c. a jacket
    b. the ocean   d. a cloud

3. What are *items* you can find in a library? Name three.

    a. _____

    b. _____

    c. _____

© Evan-Moor Corporation • EMC 2758 • Daily Academic Vocabulary   WEEK 10   47

Name_____

Day 3 group

1. How would you complete this sentence? Say it aloud.

   I would like to belong to a group that _____.

2. Which one shows a *group*? Circle your answer.

   a.   b.   c.   d.

3. Which sentence uses *group* correctly? Circle your answer.

   a. A large group of children watched the movie.
   b. I have a group of hair.
   c. Group the dirt in the hole.
   d. I am a group.

Day 4 group

1. How would you complete this sentence? Say it aloud.

   When I clean my room, I group _____ together.

2. How does a library *group* books? Circle your answers.

   a. by size of book   c. by type of book
   b. by the pictures   d. by author's last name

3. Which sentence uses *group* correctly? Circle your answer.

   a. We will group the poems by what they are about.
   b. We will group the path.
   c. Jack will group his coat.
   d. A tiger can group when it runs.

Name _____

Day 5 list • item • group

Fill in the bubble next to the correct answer.

1. A dictionary *lists* _____.

    Ⓐ words
    Ⓑ look it up
    Ⓒ many pages
    Ⓓ maps

2. What *items* do you need to brush your teeth?

    Ⓕ after every meal
    Ⓖ hairbrush and shampoo
    Ⓗ toothbrush and toothpaste
    Ⓙ twice a day

3. Which *items* belong in the same *group*?

    Ⓐ cars, trucks, kitchen
    Ⓑ jar, hairbrush, hut
    Ⓒ finger, rug, television
    Ⓓ cup, plate, fork

4. What can be *grouped* together in a zoo?

    Ⓕ big cats
    Ⓖ furniture
    Ⓗ ponds
    Ⓙ caves

My list of friends includes parrots, penguins, and peacocks!

Writing What kind of *lists* might your teacher make? What *items* could be on the *lists*? Use the words *list* and *item* in your writing.

_____

_____

_____

Daily Academic Vocabulary

WEEK 11

choose • choice

Use the reproducible definitions on page 169 and the suggestions on page 6 to introduce the words for each day.

DAY 1

choose
(verb) To pick from a group. *I choose Tess to be my reading buddy today.*

Ask: *Which fruit would you choose for a snack: a banana, an apple, or an orange? Why did you choose that fruit?* List other food groups and ask students to **choose** among them. (e.g., vegetables; drinks) Encourage students to use the word **choose** in their responses. Then conduct the first activity for Day 1 on page 51. Have students complete the Day 1 activities on their own, in pairs, or as a group.

DAY 2

choice
(noun) The thing or person that is selected. *That song was Kelsey's choice for the talent show.*

Collect and display several books from the class library. Say: *The thing we choose is our choice. I have several books here for you to choose from.* Ask: *Which book would you like to read? Which book is your choice?* Have students respond by saying, "My **choice** of book is ___." Repeat the activity several times with different students. Then conduct the first activity for Day 2 on page 51. Have students complete the Day 2 activities on their own, in pairs, or as a group.

DAY 3

choice
(noun) The right or chance to choose. *It was my choice to go to the park instead of the movies.*

Say: *Last night I had the choice to finish my book or do the dishes first. I chose to finish my book!* Ask: *What are you given a choice about?* (e.g., what to wear; games to play during free time; after-school activities) *What would you like to have a choice about?* Have students respond by saying, "I would like to have a **choice** about ___." Finally, conduct the first activity for Day 3 on page 52. Have students complete the Day 3 activities on their own, in pairs, or as a group.

DAY 4

choice
(noun) A number of things to choose or pick from. *The menu gives us a choice of vegetables.*

Say: *When there are quite a few things that we can choose or pick from, we say that there is a choice. Can you think of places or situations at school where there is a choice of things or items?* (e.g., books in the library; games to play during free time; answer choices on a test; whom to play with at recess) Then conduct the first activities for Day 4 on page 52. Have students complete the Day 4 activities on their own, in pairs, or as a group.

DAY 5

Have students complete page 53. Call on students to read aloud their answers to the writing activity.

Name _____

Day 1 choose

1. How would you complete this sentence? Say it aloud.

   At school, I get to choose _____.

2. Which phrase best completes the sentence? Circle your answer.

   The teacher chooses _____.

   a. a dinosaur to visit
   b. who will pass out the papers
   c. around the room
   d. what I wear to school

3. What would you *choose* to do this weekend?

   _____

   _____

Day 2 choice

1. How would you complete this sentence? Say it aloud.

   My choice of game to play at recess would be _____.

2. Which ones are examples of snack *choices*? Circle your answers.

   a. carrot sticks or apple slices
   b. eating
   c. cheese and crackers or a cookie
   d. health

3. Which sentence uses *choice* correctly? Circle your answer.

   a. He choice a salad.
   b. They tried to choice a healthy lunch.
   c. My choice for lunch was a turkey sandwich.
   d. Which did you choice?

© Evan-Moor Corporation • EMC 2758 • Daily Academic Vocabulary   **WEEK 11**   51

Name_____

Daily Academic Vocabulary

Day 3 choice

1. **How would you complete this sentence? Say it aloud.**

    I think children should be given a choice about _____.

2. **Finish the sentence.**

    If I had a choice, I would choose to learn about _____
    _____

3. **Which sentence uses *choice* correctly? Circle your answer.**

    a. Did you choice to do that?
    b. Sara gets to choice which movie to watch.
    c. Sara was given the choice to watch a movie instead of TV.
    d. I don't choice scary movies.

Day 4 choice

1. **How would you complete this sentence? Say it aloud.**

    I like to have a choice of _____.

2. **Which of these things gives you a *choice*? Circle your answer.**

    a. a book   c. a menu
    b. a shoe   d. a painting

3. **Which sentence uses *choice* correctly? Circle your answer.**

    a. There was a choice of animals at the pet store.
    b. We choice the two turtles.
    c. Choice pet was the favorite.
    d. There is a pet choice store at the mall.

You have a *choice* of answers!

52   **WEEK 11**   Daily Academic Vocabulary • EMC 2758 • © Evan-Moor Corporation

Name_____

Day 5 choose • choice

Fill in the bubble next to the correct answer.

1. Which one means the same as *choose*?

    Ⓐ take away

    Ⓑ pick out

    Ⓒ erase

    Ⓓ find

2. A good *choice* for breakfast is _____.

    Ⓕ 7 o'clock

    Ⓖ the breakfast table

    Ⓗ cereal, milk, toast, and juice

    Ⓙ brushing your teeth

3. Which sentence uses *choice* correctly?

    Ⓐ Jenna choice to sing.

    Ⓑ Jenna sings because she choices to do it.

    Ⓒ Do you choice to sing on stage?

    Ⓓ It is Jenna's choice to sing at the talent show.

4. Many tests contain a *choice* of _____.

    Ⓕ answers

    Ⓖ time to finish

    Ⓗ pencil and paper

    Ⓙ wrong

Writing If you could do anything this summer, what would you *choose* to do? Write about your *choices*. Use the word *choose* in your writing.

_____

_____

_____

© Evan-Moor Corporation • EMC 2758 • Daily Academic Vocabulary   **WEEK 11**   53

Daily Academic Vocabulary

WEEK 12

appear • appearance

Use the reproducible definitions on page 170 and the suggestions on page 6 to introduce the words for each day.

DAY 1

appear
(verb) To seem to be. Sometimes things **appear** to be different than they really are.

Hold up a globe. Say: *You know that this globe is a model of the Earth. What shape is it?* (round; sphere) *But when we look at the Earth from where we are, it does not **appear** round. It seems to be flat; it **appears** to be flat.* Then ask: *Are there times when you have **appeared** to be different from what you really are?* (e.g., in costume for a play; at Halloween) Encourage students to use the word **appear** in their responses. Conduct the first activity for Day 1 on page 55. Have students complete the Day 1 activities on their own, in pairs, or as a group.

DAY 2

appear
(verb) To come into view. The sun will **appear** from behind the clouds.

Explain that the word **appears** means you can see something that might have been hidden or not there before. Ask: *After it rains, what colorful thing **appears** in the sky?* (a rainbow) Then conduct the first activity for Day 2 on page 55. Have students complete the Day 2 activities on their own, in pairs, or as a group.

DAY 3

appearance
(noun) The act of coming into view. A clown made an **appearance** at the party.

Point out that when something or someone appears, it's called an **appearance**. Hold a puppet or small object out of view, and then hold it up for students to see. Ask: *What (or who) just made an **appearance**?* Ask students to name people that make an **appearance** in their classroom for special events. (e.g., principal; guest speaker) Then conduct the first activity for Day 3 on page 56. Have students complete the Day 3 activities on their own, in pairs, or as a group.

DAY 4

appearance
(noun) The way that something or somebody looks. The **appearance** of the school was clean and neat.

Choose two books, a new one and an old, worn one. Have students compare the **appearance** of the two books. Ask: *How would you describe the **appearance** of these books?* Next, choose two areas of the classroom, such as one that is cluttered and one that is not. Ask students to describe the **appearance** of each area. Then conduct the first activity for Day 4 on page 56. Have students complete the Day 4 activities on their own, in pairs, or as a group.

DAY 5

Have students complete page 57. Call on students to read aloud their answers to the writing activity.

Name_____

Day 1 appear

1. How would you complete this sentence? Say it aloud.

   I try to appear brave when _____.

2. Which word best completes the sentence? Circle your answer.

   Did it rain last night? The ground appears _____.

   a. find   c. wet
   b. sad   d. seems

3. If a lion *appeared* to be hungry, what would it be doing? Circle your answer.

   a. playing
   b. sleeping
   c. snoring
   d. looking for food

Day 2 appear

1. How would you complete this sentence? Say it aloud.

   I will close my eyes, open them, and wish for _____ to appear.

2. Which of these would <u>never</u> *appear* in the night sky? Circle your answers.

   a. the sun   c. moon
   b. stars   d. a rainbow

3. Which sentence uses *appear* correctly? Circle your answer.

   a. Will the full moon appear tonight?
   b. I can see the appear of a full moon.
   c. The full moon will be appear.
   d. The full moon appears when it hides.

Name_____

Day 3 appearance

1. How would you complete this sentence? Say it aloud.

    I would be really excited if _____ made an appearance in our town!

2. What does it mean when someone makes an *appearance*? Circle your answer.

    a. The person shows up.
    b. The person orders dinner.
    c. The person sleeps over.
    d. The person goes away.

3. Which sentence uses *appearance* correctly? Circle your answer.

    a. The appearance donkey made us laugh.
    b. The appearance laughed at the donkey.
    c. We felt an appearance with a donkey.
    d. The appearance of the donkey made us laugh.

Day 4 appearance

1. How would you complete this sentence? Say it aloud.

    The appearance of my room is usually _____.

2. How can someone keep a clean *appearance*? Circle your answers.

    a. go hiking every day
    b. wash every day
    c. wear clean clothes
    d. play outside

3. Which word best describes the *appearance* of a ball without air in it? Circle your answer.

    a. flat   c. fat
    b. round   d. bouncing

56   **WEEK 12**   Daily Academic Vocabulary • EMC 2758 • © Evan-Moor Corporation

Name_____

Daily Academic Vocabulary

Day 5 appear • appearance

Fill in the bubble next to the correct answer.

1. **Which word means almost the same thing as *appears*?**
    - Ⓐ seems
    - Ⓑ likeness
    - Ⓒ likely
    - Ⓓ finds

2. **Which ones might *appear* in a tree?**
    - Ⓕ trees
    - Ⓖ stars
    - Ⓗ birds
    - Ⓙ rain

3. **Which one does the opposite of making an *appearance*?**
    - Ⓐ A chick comes out of its shell.
    - Ⓑ A frog jumps out of the water.
    - Ⓒ The moon hides behind a cloud.
    - Ⓓ A star shines in the sky.

4. **Which one best completes this sentence?**

    Tino _____ to keep his room's neat *appearance*.
    - Ⓕ sleeps late on Saturday
    - Ⓖ puts away his clothes and toys
    - Ⓗ makes breakfast
    - Ⓙ plays the trumpet

Writing Who would you like to make an *appearance* at a school assembly? Why? Use the word *appearance* in your writing.

_____

_____

Daily Academic Vocabulary

WEEK 13

image • imagine
imagination • imaginary

Use the reproducible definitions on page 171 and the suggestions on page 6 to introduce the words for each day.

DAY 1

image
(noun) A picture of a person or thing. *The painting shows an image of a horse racing across a desert.*

(noun) A picture of something in the mind. *When I think of summer, the image of the beach comes to my mind.*

Show students pictures in a book. Ask: *What images do you see in this book?* Explain that **images**, pictures of people or things, help illustrate a story, an ad, or an article. They explain something more about the words. Then say: *Now close your eyes and make a picture in your mind. It has red petals and a long green stem. It smells very sweet.* Tell students to open their eyes. Ask: *What image did you see in your mind?* Then conduct the first activity for Day 1 on page 59. Have students complete the Day 1 activities on their own, in pairs, or as a group.

DAY 2

imagine
(verb) To picture something in your mind. *Sometimes I imagine that I am an astronaut on Mars.*

Say: *When authors write stories, they sometimes imagine things that don't really happen. Can you think of any examples of this from stories you know?* Encourage students to use the word **imagined** in their responses. (e.g., "In the story ___, the author **imagined** that ___.") Then conduct the first activity for Day 2 on page 59. Have students complete the Day 2 activities on their own, in pairs, or as a group.

DAY 3

imagination
(noun) The talent to picture things in the mind. *Ramon's stories show what a good imagination he has.*

Display or mention a fantasy book that your students know well, such as *Dogzilla* by Dav Pilkey, *Jumanji* by Chris Van Allsburg, or the *Harry Potter* series by J. K. Rowling. Ask: *How did the author use his or her imagination to create this story? How do you use your imagination when you write stories or pretend?* Then conduct the first activity for Day 3 on page 60. Have students complete the Day 3 activities on their own, in pairs, or as a group.

DAY 4

imaginary
(adj.) Not real. *An elf is an imaginary creature.*

Ask: *Is (Cinderella, Mickey Mouse, Peter Pan, etc.) a real or imaginary person? What other imaginary people or animals have you seen in cartoons or movies or read about in books? What makes them imaginary?* Then conduct the first activity for Day 4 on page 60. Have students complete the Day 4 activities on their own, in pairs, or as a group.

DAY 5

Have students complete page 61. Call on students to read aloud their answers to the writing activity.

Name_____

Day 1 image

1. How would you complete this sentence? Say it aloud.

   I could make an image of _____ using _____.

2. Which one makes *images*? Circle your answer.

   a. a camera
   b. a box
   c. a piece of paper
   d. a carton

3. What *image* comes to mind when you notice good smells from the kitchen? Circle your answer.

   a. doing homework
   b. washing clothes
   c. going to bed
   d. something yummy

Day 2 imagine

1. How would you complete this sentence? Say it aloud.

   I like to imagine that _____.

2. Which one tells what the word *imagine* means? Circle your answer.

   a. to know something is true
   b. to write about something
   c. to sing a song about something
   d. to picture what something might be like

3. Which sentence uses *imagine* correctly? Circle your answer.

   a. My camera imagines what you look like.
   b. His new computer can imagine what's in my head.
   c. I like to imagine what I could do with a million dollars.
   d. I have a new imagine.

© Evan-Moor Corporation • EMC 2758 • Daily Academic Vocabulary **WEEK 13** 59

Name_____

Daily Academic Vocabulary

Day 3 imagination

1. How would you complete this sentence? Say it aloud.

   The best thing about having an imagination is _____.

2. When would an *imagination* be the most useful? Circle your answer.

   a. when telling the facts about something
   b. when writing a make-believe story
   c. when following directions for a science experiment
   d. when taking a spelling test

3. Which sentence uses *imagination* correctly? Circle your answer.

   a. I will find the imagination in the drawer.
   b. Robbie imaginations it.
   c. An imagination was inside the book.
   d. When it thunders, my imagination sees giants fighting in the sky.

Day 4 imaginary

1. How would you complete this sentence? Say it aloud.

   I would like to visit an imaginary place where _____.

2. Which animal is *imaginary*? Circle your answer.

a.   b.   c.   d.

3. Which one means the opposite of *imaginary*? Circle your answer.

   a. real
   b. make-believe
   c. made up
   d. doesn't exist in real life

WEEK 13

Name_____

Day 5 image • imagine
imagination • imaginary

Daily
Academic
Vocabulary

Fill in the bubble next to the correct answer.

1. Where would *images* be found?
    - Ⓐ on a blank page
    - Ⓑ on a television screen
    - Ⓒ in ice cream
    - Ⓓ in a dark closet

2. What *image* do most people see when they hear a bark?
    - Ⓕ a tree
    - Ⓖ a cat
    - Ⓗ a train
    - Ⓙ a dog

3. Which sentence uses *imagines* correctly?
    - Ⓐ Imagines is a good thing to use.
    - Ⓑ Mia has a good imagines.
    - Ⓒ Mia imagines being a movie star.
    - Ⓓ Mia always likes to imagines.

4. An artist may use his or her *imagination* to _____.
    - Ⓕ paint a picture
    - Ⓖ clean up after painting
    - Ⓗ hold a brush
    - Ⓙ put paint on the brush

Writing Write about an *imaginary* character you would like to meet. Use the word *imagine* or *imaginary* in your writing.

_____

_____

_____

Daily Academic Vocabulary

WEEK 14

invent • invention
create • creation

Use the reproducible definitions on page 172 and the suggestions on page 6 to introduce the words for each day.

DAY 1

invent
(verb) To make up or think of something new. *Someone might invent a flying car.*

Say: *People often invent things to make life easier or to solve a problem.* Show students a stapler. Ask: *Why did someone invent the stapler?* (e.g., to hold papers together; to keep them from getting separated) Point to or show students other objects, such as a pencil, a doorknob, a light, or a clock. Ask students why someone wanted to **invent** each thing. Conduct the first activity for Day 1 on page 63. Then have students complete the Day 1 activities on their own, in pairs, or as a group.

DAY 2

invention
(noun) Something that is invented. *The computer is a useful invention.*

Say: *Some inventions are very simple. Others have a lot of parts.* Show students a pencil and a computer, or other machine. Ask: *Which invention has only one part? Which invention has a lot of parts?* Then ask: *What things in this room are not inventions?* (e.g., people; plants; rocks) Then conduct the first activity for Day 2 on page 63. Have students complete the Day 2 activities on their own, in pairs, or as a group.

DAY 3

create
(verb) To make or design something. *An artist can create a painting.*

(verb) To cause to happen. *The baby will create a mess with her food.*

Have students think about an upcoming school event, such as a bake sale or play. Ask: *How could you create or design a poster for the event?* (e.g., use markers and cardboard) *How might making the poster create or cause a mess?* Then conduct the first activity for Day 3 on page 64. Have students complete the Day 3 activities on their own, in pairs, or as a group.

DAY 4

creation
(noun) Something that has been made. *Ana's favorite creation is a model volcano she made last year.*

Read a short poem to the class. Say: *That poem is the creation of the writer. A poem is a creation made with words. A painting is a creation made with art supplies. Creations can be made from many things. What creations have you made at school this year?* (e.g., paintings; stories; collages) Then conduct the first activity for Day 4 on page 64. Have students complete the Day 4 activities on their own, in pairs, or as a group.

DAY 5

Have students complete page 65. Call on students to read aloud their answers to the writing activity.

Name_____

Day 1 invent

1. **How would you complete this sentence? Say it aloud.**

   I would like to invent a machine that _____.

2. **Which sentence uses *invent* correctly? Circle your answer.**

   a. The telephone is a useful invent.
   b. I want to invent a new game.
   c. Her invent did not work right away.
   d. The trees invent falling leaves.

3. **What do you need in order to *invent* something? Circle your answer.**

   a. a factory   c. an idea
   b. a scientist   d. a machine

Day 2 invention

1. **How would you complete this sentence? Say it aloud.**

   I think _____ is a great invention.

2. **Which of these are *inventions*? Circle your answers.**

   a.   b.   c.   d.

3. **What do all *inventions* have in common? Circle your answer.**

   a. They are made of metal.
   b. People ride in them.
   c. Someone thought of each one.
   d. They all have many small parts.

WEEK 14

Name_____

Day 3 create

1. How would you complete these sentences? Say them aloud.

   I can use paper to create a _____.

   I try not to create a mess in _____.

2. Which sentence uses *create* correctly? Circle your answer.

   a. Words that rhyme can help you create a poem.
   b. They create a kitten for their brother.
   c. The create problem is very hard to solve.
   d. My favorite create is a song I wrote last year.

3. What can a lot of rain *create*? Circle your answer.

   a. ice
   b. snow
   c. a flood
   d. umbrellas

Day 4 creation

1. How would you complete this sentence? Say it aloud.

   My best creation was _____.

2. What is one *creation* of a writer? Circle your answer.

   a. a pencil
   b. a lamp
   c. a desk
   d. a book

3. Which sentence means that the quilt was Koji's *creation*? Circle your answer.

   a. Koji sewed the quilt by hand.
   b. Koji slept with the quilt every night.
   c. Koji liked the pattern on the quilt.
   d. Koji's grandmother gave him the quilt.

Name_____

Day 5 invent • invention • create • creation

Fill in the bubble next to the correct answer.

1. When you *invent* something, what do you make?
   - Ⓐ something big
   - Ⓑ something strange
   - Ⓒ something impossible
   - Ⓓ something new *(circled)*

2. Which of these is an *invention*?
   - Ⓕ a flower
   - Ⓖ a bicycle *(circled)*
   - Ⓗ a rabbit
   - Ⓙ the sun

3. What can a bird *create*?
   - Ⓐ a feather
   - Ⓑ a nest *(circled)*
   - Ⓒ a tree
   - Ⓓ wings

4. Why is a story a *creation*?
   - Ⓕ It is very short.
   - Ⓖ People read it. *(circled)*
   - Ⓗ It has words in it.
   - Ⓙ Somebody made it up.

My nest is the best **creation**!

Writing   Think about an art project. What would you like to *create*? What is one *invention* you will use to *create* it? Use the words *create* and *invention* in your writing.

My noodles are the best creaiton!

Daily Academic Vocabulary

WEEK 15

solve • solution
figure • figure out

Use the reproducible definitions on page 173 and the suggestions on page 6 to introduce the words for each day.

DAY 1

solve
(verb) To find an answer to a problem. *Tamara will **solve** the math problem by adding two numbers together.*

Write this problem on the board: 5 + 7 = ? Ask: *How can you **solve** this problem?* (Add the numbers to find the sum.) Point out that we **solve** many different kinds of problems every day. Say: *Josh has a problem. He keeps forgetting to bring his homework to school. How can Josh **solve** his problem?* Discuss possible ways to **solve** the problem. (e.g., write notes; ask someone to remind him) Then conduct the first activity for Day 1 on page 67. Have students complete the Day 1 activities on their own, in pairs, or as a group.

DAY 2

solution
(noun) The answer to a problem. *I found the **solution** to the word problem by using subtraction.*

Say: *A **solution** is the answer to a problem. You often see this word in math when we talk about the answers to math problems. However, **solution** can be used as the answer to any kind of problem. What would be the **solution** to a messy room? To a hungry stomach?* Conduct the first activity for Day 2 on page 67. Have students complete the Day 2 activities on their own, in pairs, or as a group.

DAY 3

figure
(verb) To work something out by using numbers. *I will **figure** the cost of our lunch on my calculator.*

figure out
(verb) To solve something by thinking about it. *I know you can **figure out** the riddle if you keep working on it.*

Ask: *How can you **figure** the number of minutes we spend reading each day?* (count the minutes) *How can you **figure** the number of students in our school?* (count them; add the classes) Say: *When you **figure** something, you work out a problem by using numbers.* Then say, *Sometimes you would say **figure out** instead of **figure**.* Repeat the first two sentences above, replacing **figure** with **figure out**. Then say: *When you **figure out** something, you don't have to use numbers. How can we **figure out** what is for lunch today?* Then conduct the first activity for Day 3 on page 68. Have students complete the Day 3 activities on their own, in pairs, or as a group.

DAY 4

figure
(noun) An outline, form, or shape. *I see the **figure** of a crouching lion in the cloud.*

Show or draw for students a ball, a box, and a pencil. Ask: *If we place each of these things in front of a light, which one will cast a shadow that makes the **figure** of a circle?* Allow students to experiment to check their answers, if possible. Then conduct the first activity for Day 4 on page 68. Have students complete the Day 4 activities on their own, in pairs, or as a group.

DAY 5

Have students complete page 69. Call on students to read aloud their answers to the writing activity.

Name_____

Daily Academic Vocabulary

Day 1 solve

1. **How would you complete this sentence? Say it aloud.**

   One problem my class worked together to solve was _____.

2. **Which of the following can you *solve*? Circle your answers.**

   a. a computer   c. a mystery
   b. a riddle   d. a house

3. **What happens if you help your family *solve* a problem? Circle your answer.**

   a. The problem is fixed.
   b. Your family gets angry.
   c. The problem gets bigger.
   d. The problem stays the same.

Day 2 solution

1. **How would you complete this sentence? Say it aloud.**

   I helped find a solution to _____.

2. **Which of the following does not use *solution* correctly? Circle your answer.**

   a. Megan used multiplication to find the solution to the problem.
   b. One solution is to plant more trees.
   c. What is your solution?
   d. Can you solution the problem for me?

3. **In which sentence does someone find a *solution*? Circle your answer.**

   a. Jalisa loves her dance and music lessons.
   b. Callie figured out how to send an e-mail.
   c. Adia decided to write her book report.
   d. Aiden wants to learn how to fly a plane.

© Evan-Moor Corporation • EMC 2758 • Daily Academic Vocabulary   WEEK 15   67

Name _____

Daily Academic Vocabulary

Day 3 figure • figure out

1. How would you complete these sentences? Say them aloud.

   I can figure the amount of time I _____ by _____.

   When I am reading a book, I try to figure out _____.

2. What would you do to *figure* how tall a building is? Circle your answer.

   a. look at the building
   b. count the number of floors
   c. walk around the building
   d. draw the building

3. In which sentence does someone *figure out* something? Circle your answer.

   a. Farida took a photograph of her pet hamster.
   b. Howard borrowed a pencil from Tony.
   c. Leo discovered how the magic trick was done.
   d. Alicia won a spelling contest.

Day 4 figure

1. How would you complete this sentence? Say it aloud.

   I can use modeling clay to make a figure of _____.

2. Which of these things are round *figures*? Circle your answers.

a.   b.   c.   d.

3. Which words can describe a *figure*? Circle your answers.

   a. shy   c. sneaky
   b. round   d. thin

Name_____

Day 5 solve • solution • figure • figure out

Daily Academic Vocabulary

Fill in the bubble next to the correct answer.

1. Which sentence describes someone who *solves* something?

Ⓐ Billie knows the name of every president.
Ⓑ Alex writes a letter to his best friend.
Ⓒ Hector plays soccer on Saturdays.
Ⓓ Keisha finds the answer to a hard problem.

2. In which sentence does someone *figure* a price?

Ⓕ The price of the toy was six dollars plus tax.
Ⓖ Joel asked the price of the bicycle.
Ⓗ Emily found the total price of the doll by adding the tax.
Ⓙ Jonathan paid the price of ten dollars.

3. What do you need to do to *figure out* a problem?

Ⓐ think about it
Ⓑ write numbers around it
Ⓒ keep away from it
Ⓓ stop it from happening

4. Which of the following has the same *figure* as a rectangle?

Ⓕ a postage stamp
Ⓖ a pair of scissors
Ⓗ a round rug
Ⓙ a flower

Writing Tell about a problem you had to *solve*. What was your *solution*? Use the words *solve* and *solution* in your writing.

_____

_____

_____

© Evan-Moor Corporation • EMC 2758 • Daily Academic Vocabulary   **WEEK 15**

Daily Academic Vocabulary

WEEK 16

amount • measure
measures • measurement

Use the reproducible definitions on page 174 and the suggestions on page 6 to introduce the words for each day.

DAY 1

amount
(noun) How much there is of something. *The amount of flour you need to make the cake is 4 cups.*

Show students two stacks of paper, one obviously larger than the other. Say: *Which stack has the larger amount of paper?* Then show two paper bags of different sizes. Ask: *Which of these bags will hold the larger amount of groceries?* Then ask: *What is the amount of time left in this class (or school) day?* Then conduct the first activity for Day 1 on page 71. Have students complete the Day 1 activities on their own, in pairs, or as a group.

DAY 2

measure
(verb) To find the length, size, weight, or amount of something. *Will you measure my height?*

Show students a box. Ask: *How many different ways can you think of to measure this box?* (e.g., use a ruler or tape measure to find length, width, and height; weigh it) Ask: *Why do we measure things?* (to know if something is the right size or amount; to know how much we have) Encourage students to use the word **measure** in their responses. Then conduct the first activity for Day 2 on page 71. Have students complete the Day 2 activities on their own, in pairs, or as a group.

DAY 3

measures
(verb) To provide a way of measuring. *A thermometer measures temperature.*

Ask: *What tools do we use to measure things?* (rulers; scales; clocks; thermometers) Then ask: *What does a ruler measure?* Say: *That's correct, a ruler measures the length of something.* Have students use the word **measures** to describe other measurement tools. Then conduct the first activity for Day 3 on page 72. Have students complete the Day 3 activities on their own, in pairs, or as a group.

DAY 4

measurement
(noun) The length, size, weight, or amount of something. *Please take an exact measurement of the window.*

Say: *The word measurement is used to describe several things. What kind of measurement would be given in pounds?* (weight) *In seconds?* (time) *In feet?* (length or height) Ask students: *When might we need to find the measurement of something?* Encourage them to use the word **measurement** in their responses. Then conduct the first activity for Day 4 on page 72. Have students complete the Day 4 activities on their own, in pairs, or as a group.

DAY 5

Have students complete page 73. Call on students to read aloud their answers to the writing activity.

Name _____

Day 1 amount

1. How would you complete this sentence? Say it aloud.

   The amount of time I need to do my homework is _____.

2. Which of the following might you want to know the *amount* of? Circle your answers.

   a. a TV show
   b. rainfall in a year
   c. a social studies lesson
   d. sugar needed to make cookies

3. Which sentence uses *amount* correctly? Circle your answer.

   a. We will amount the rain that falls.
   b. The amount of water in the lake is less in the summer.
   c. Our class can amount things with a ruler or a scale.
   d. There is too much amount of red in the painting.

Day 2 measure

1. How would you complete this sentence? Say it aloud.

   I could measure the height of this room by _____.

2. Which of the following *measure* things? Circle your answers.

   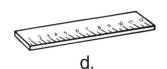

   a.   b.   c.   d.

3. Which sentences describe someone *measuring* something? Circle your answers.

   a. Nori put some apples on the scale.
   b. Mike brings a dozen markers to school.
   c. Crystal finds the length of her desk.
   d. Van remembers more than fifty songs.

Name_____

Daily Academic Vocabulary

Day 3 measures

1. How would you complete this sentence? Say it aloud.

   The clock in our classroom measures _____.

2. Which of these *measure* length? Circle your answers.

   a. the hour hand on a clock   c. a meter stick
   b. a yardstick   d. your math book

3. Which sentence uses *measures* correctly?
   Circle your answer.

   a. My watch measures hours, minutes, and seconds.
   b. We will measures the length of the bookcase.
   c. A pencil measures paper.
   d. Weight measures a scale.

Day 4 measurement

1. How would you complete this sentence? Say it aloud.

   I would like to take the measurement of the _____.

2. Which of the following are *measurements*?
   Circle your answers.

   a. 7 yards   c. 18 seconds
   b. horses in a barn   d. 10 cats

3. How can you find the *measurement* of a line?
   Circle your answer.

   a. Draw a copy of it on a piece of paper.
   b. Use a stick to find out if it is straight.
   c. Use a ruler to find out how long it is.
   d. Fold it in half and cut it into two parts.

72   WEEK 16

Name_____

Day 5 | amount • measure
measures • measurement

Daily Academic Vocabulary

Fill in the bubble next to the correct answer.

1. What do you know if you find out the *amount* of something?

    Ⓐ where it comes from

    Ⓑ how much of it there is

    Ⓒ who it belongs to

    Ⓓ how old it is

2. What is one tool we use to *measure* something?

    Ⓕ glue

    Ⓖ a pair of scissors

    Ⓗ pencil

    Ⓙ a clock

3. What is something a scale *measures*?

    Ⓐ pounds

    Ⓑ inches

    Ⓒ degrees

    Ⓓ minutes

4. Which sentence uses *measurement* correctly?

    Ⓕ The length of this room measurements 27 feet.

    Ⓖ You can measurement a wall with a yardstick.

    Ⓗ The rug is two yards measurement.

    Ⓙ The measurement of the water in the bucket is one gallon.

Writing   Choose something to *measure*. Tell how you will *measure* it. Guess what the *measurement* will be. Use the words *measure* and *measurement* in your writing.

_____

_____

_____

Daily Academic Vocabulary

WEEK 17

improve • improvement
success • successful

Use the reproducible definitions on page 175 and the suggestions on page 6 to introduce the words for each day.

DAY 1

improve
(verb) To get better, or to make something better. *He will improve his story if he adds a surprise ending.*

Write this sentence on the board: "The catz likes millk." Ask: *How can we improve this sentence? How can we make it better?* (The cats like milk.) Say: *You can improve situations. You can improve something you do. If you wanted to be a better speller, how could you improve?* (learn spelling rules; practice; read) Conduct the first activity for Day 1 on page 75. Have students complete the Day 1 activities on their own, in pairs, or as a group.

DAY 2

improvement
(noun) A change that makes something better. *Painting the wall yellow will be a great improvement.*

Ask: *What is an improvement we could make to our school or classroom? How can we make it better?* Then say: *Sometimes you need time to see an improvement. You might see one in a few moments, or it might take weeks, months, or years.* Ask: *What improvements could take a long time to see?* (in reading; buildings) Conduct the first activity for Day 2 on page 75. Then have students complete the Day 2 activities on their own, in pairs, or as a group.

DAY 3

success
(noun) A person who does well, or something that goes well. *Rob's science experiment was a success.*

Ask: *What makes something a success?* After a brief discussion, place a tissue or feather on a table or desk. Say: *I am going to try to blow this tissue (or feather) off the table. Will it be a success?* Allow students to answer. Blow the tissue (or feather) off the table. Then say: *It was a success! I was able to blow the tissue (or feather) off the table. I am a success because I blew the tissue (or feather) off the table.* Then conduct the first activity for Day 3 on page 76. Have students complete the Day 3 activities on their own, in pairs, or as a group.

DAY 4

successful
(adj.) Ending or going well; having success. *The students were successful in learning their spelling words.*

Say: *Tell me whether each sentence I say tells something that is successful or something that is not successful. Roberto repaired the flat tire on his bike. Janna did not make the finals of the singing contest. The cake we baked was dry and tasteless. Dad got a new job.* Then ask: *What are you successful in?* Have students respond by saying, "I am successful in ___." Then conduct the first activity for Day 4 on page 76. Have students complete the Day 4 activities on their own, in pairs, or as a group.

DAY 5

Have students complete page 77. Call on students to read aloud their answers to the writing activity.

Name_____

Daily Academic Vocabulary

Day 1 improve

1. **How would you complete this sentence? Say it aloud.**

   My schoolwork will improve if I _____.

2. **How can you *improve* a long car trip? Circle your answers.**

   a. Think of a game to play while riding in the car.
   b. Don't take the trip.
   c. Bring something interesting to read.
   d. Have a fight about where to go.

3. **Which of the following can *improve* when you practice? Circle your answers.**

   a. how old you are
   b. drum playing
   c. how tall you are
   d. swimming

Day 2 improvement

1. **How would you complete this sentence? Say it aloud.**

   If I practice every day, there will be an improvement in my _____.

2. **Which sentence describes someone who makes an *improvement*? Circle your answer.**

   a. Paula remembers her favorite vacation.
   b. Jared repairs a broken toy for his brother.
   c. Evan knows how to play the violin.
   d. Badra plays a game with her little sister.

3. **When will you see an *improvement*? Circle your answer.**

   a. when somebody gets better at something
   b. when somebody gets worse at something
   c. when somebody gives a wrong answer
   d. when somebody takes a long time to do something

Name _____

Day 3 success

1. How would you complete this sentence? Say it aloud.

   I hope to be a success in _____.

2. Which sentence does not use *success* correctly? Circle your answer.

   a. Morgan was a success when he did not do his homework.
   b. The play was a success because everyone loved it.
   c. The team found success when they won the game.
   d. Maeve's success came about because she worked hard.

3. Which of the following describes a *success*? Circle your answers.

   a. The rocket took off into space.
   b. The rocket was not able to take off.
   c. A piece of the rocket fell off.
   d. The rocket landed on the moon.

Day 4 successful

1. How would you complete this sentence? Say it aloud.

   I can be successful in school by _____.

2. What can help a person be *successful*? Circle your answer.

   a. giving up   c. working hard
   b. not trying   d. not caring

3. Which sentence uses *successful* correctly? Circle your answer.

   a. The successful store never sold anything.
   b. I am a successful in math.
   c. My mother gave me a successful.
   d. The successful restaurant was always busy.

76   **WEEK 17**   Daily Academic Vocabulary • EMC 2758 • © Evan-Moor Corporation

Name_____

Day 5 | improve • improvement
success • successful

Daily Academic Vocabulary

Fill in the bubble next to the correct answer.

1. How can you *improve* a story?

  Ⓐ Correct any mistakes.
  Ⓑ Throw it away.
  Ⓒ Give it to a friend.
  Ⓓ Take out all of the words.

2. What do all *improvements* have in common?

  Ⓕ They make something longer.
  Ⓖ They make something easier.
  Ⓗ They make something better.
  Ⓙ They make something prettier.

3. A *success* is always something that is done _____.

  Ⓐ badly
  Ⓑ over a long time
  Ⓒ in a different way
  Ⓓ well

4. If something is *successful*, it _____.

  Ⓕ is different
  Ⓖ needs to be changed
  Ⓗ is going well
  Ⓙ is going badly

Writing What is something you would like to *improve*? How will you know when you have made an *improvement*? Use the words *improve* and *improvement* in your writing.

© Evan-Moor Corporation • EMC 2758 • Daily Academic Vocabulary **WEEK 17**

CUMULATIVE REVIEW
WORDS FROM WEEKS 10–17

amount
appear
appearance
choice
choose
create
creation
figure
figure out
group
image
imaginary
imagination
imagine
improve
improvement
invent
invention
item
list
measure
measurement
measures
solution
solve
success
successful

Days 1–4
Each day's activity is a cloze paragraph that students complete with words or forms of words that they have learned in weeks 10–17. Before students begin, pronounce each word in the box on the student page, have students repeat each word, and then review each word's meaning(s). **Other ways to review the words:**

- Start a sentence containing one of the words and have students finish the sentence orally. For example:

    *If I could **choose** to be a character in a story, I would **choose**…*
    *I wish that somebody would **invent** a machine that…*

- Provide students with a definition and ask them to supply the word that fits it.
- Ask questions that require students to know the meaning of each word. For example:

    *Give me one example of an **imaginary** animal.*
    *What are some of the things students often **create** at school?*
    *What can you **measure** with a thermometer?*

- Have students use each word in a sentence.

Day 5
Start by reviewing the five words not practiced on Days 1–4: **amount, creation, image, invent, solution**. Write the words on the board and have students repeat them after you. Provide a sentence for one of the words. Ask students to think of their own sentence and share it with a partner. Call on several students to share their sentences. Follow the same procedure for the remaining words. Then have students complete the code-breaker activity.

Extension Ideas
Use any of the following activities to help integrate the vocabulary words into other content areas:

- Have students **create** an **imaginary** creature in clay. Then have them write a story about what would happen if the creature **appeared** at school.
- Ask students to make a **list** of **inventions** they use every day. Ask them to explain how each **invention improves** their lives.
- Learn about water conservation. Use one gallon to represent the **amount** of water on Earth. **Measure** and pour ½ cup into another container. This represents all the fresh water on Earth. Use your finger or an eyedropper to remove two drops from the ½ cup. This is the **amount** of water available for our use. Ask how students can reduce their water usage.
- Have students **measure** each other's height and plot it on a class chart. Repeat the activity at the end of the year and compare **measurements**.

Name _____

| appearance | figure out | imagination | improve | success |
| choose | group | imagine | invention | successful |

Day 1

Fill in the blanks with words from the word box.

Sometimes the look, or _____, of something can fool you. Did you know that a tomato is a fruit and not a vegetable? Scientists place it in the same _____ as berries. Of course, tomatoes are not as sweet as blueberries or strawberries. Can you _____ eating tomato ice cream? I think I would _____ a different flavor!

Day 2

Fill in the blanks with words from the word box.

The zipper is a very useful _____. It can close things more tightly than buttons. In 1858, Elias Howe tried to _____ a way to make clothing better. He wanted to _____ the way clothing stayed closed. Sadly, his creation was not a _____. Then in 1913, Gideon Sundback used his _____ to make the first working zipper. He was _____!

Name_____

Daily Academic Vocabulary

| appears | create | imaginary | item | measure | solve |
| choice | figure | improvement | list | measurement | |

Day 3

Fill in the blanks with words from the word box.

Here's a problem that you can _____. Suppose that you want to _____ how high a door is. What will you do first? You can begin by making a _____ of the steps you will follow. What tools will you use? You might use a ruler. Another handy _____ you can use is a yardstick. How can you be sure that your _____ is correct?

Day 4

Fill in the blanks with words from the word box.

An artist can use clay to _____ different shapes. First, she makes a _____ about what to make. She might make a vase that has the shape, or _____, of a cube. Or she might decide to make a vase that _____ to be an _____ animal or a person. After the clay dries, she can still make changes. She might make an _____ with sandpaper or a file. These will make the outside of the vase smoother.

Name _____

Day 5

Crack the Code!

Write one of the words from the word box on the lines below each clue.

amount	create	image	improve	item	solution
appear	creation	imaginary	improvement	list	success
appearance	figure	imagination	invent	measure	successful
choice	figure out	imagine	invention	measurement	solve
choose	group				

1. something that has been made

   ___ ___ ___ ___ ___ ___ ___ ___
     1   2

2. how much there is of something

   ___ ___ ___ ___ ___ ___
     3

3. to think of something new

   ___ ___ ___ ___ ___ ___
             4

4. a picture of something

   ___ ___ ___ ___
     5

5. the answer to a problem

   ___ ___ ___ ___ ___ ___ ___ ___
     6

6. to make something better

   ___ ___ ___ ___ ___ ___ ___
         7

Now use the numbers under the letters to crack the code. Write the letters on the lines below. The words will answer this riddle.

What do you use to fix a broken tomato?

___ ___ ___ ___ ___ ___ ___ ___ ___ ___ ___
 4   2   5   3   4   2   7   3   6   4   1

© Evan-Moor Corporation • EMC 2758 • Daily Academic Vocabulary

Daily Academic Vocabulary

WEEK 19

different • similar
compare • comparison

Use the reproducible definitions on page 176 and the suggestions on page 6 to introduce the words for each day.

DAY 1

different
(adj.) Not the same; unlike something else. *My sister's straight hair is very **different** from my curly hair.*

Draw a triangle and a square on the board. Ask: *How are these two shapes **different**?* (One has four sides and corners; the other has three.) Add a circle and a rectangle to the board. Ask: *Which of these four shapes do you think is the most **different**? Why?* (The circle because it does not have straight sides.) Then conduct the first activity for Day 1 on page 83. Have students complete the Day 1 activities on their own, in pairs, or as a group.

DAY 2

similar
(adj.) Alike but not exactly the same as something else. *A baseball is **similar** to a softball, except it is smaller.*

Ask: *How are a television and a computer **similar**?* Encourage students to use the word **similar** in their responses. Emphasize that two things are **similar** when they are alike but not exactly the same. Say: *Two pencils might be exactly the same. A pencil and a pen are **similar**. They are both used for writing, but they are not exactly the same.* Ask: *What are two other things that are **similar**? How are they **similar**?* Then conduct the first activity for Day 2 on page 83. Have students complete the Day 2 activities on their own, in pairs, or as a group.

DAY 3

compare
(verb) To judge how two or more things are different and alike. *I will **compare** the two shirts before I decide which one to buy.*

Show students a pencil, a marker, and a crayon. Ask: *How can we **compare** these three things?* Say: *When we **compare**, we often use the words "similar" and "different."* Encourage students to identify things the items have in common and things that are different. Point out that we usually **compare** things that have something in common. Ask: *Why might it be difficult to **compare** an elephant and a flashlight?* Conduct the first activity for Day 3 on page 84. Then have students complete the Day 3 activities on their own, in pairs, or as a group.

DAY 4

comparison
(noun) The act of judging how two or more things are different and alike. *A quick **comparison** shows me that this book is longer than that one.*

Ask students to compare two stories you have recently read in class. Compare the plot, the setting, and the main characters. After a brief discussion, say: *We have just made a **comparison** of two stories.* Then ask: *How does making a **comparison** help you better understand both books?* Then conduct the first activity for Day 4 on page 84. Have students complete the Day 4 activities on their own, in pairs, or as a group.

DAY 5

Have students complete page 85. Call on students to read aloud their answers to the writing activity.

Name _____

Day 1 different

1. How would you complete this sentence? Say it aloud.

   Addition is different from subtraction because _____.

2. How are a duck and a sheep *different*? Circle your answers.

   a. They are both animals that can live on farms.
   b. A duck can fly and a sheep cannot.
   c. A duck has feathers and a sheep has wool.
   d. Neither one can be a pet in the city.

3. Which of the following have shapes very *different* from an orange? Circle your answers.

   a. a grapefruit   c. a pineapple
   b. a grape   d. a banana

Day 2 similar

1. How would you complete this sentence? Say it aloud.

   A _____ is similar to a horse.

2. Which of these things are *similar*? Circle your answers.

a.   b.   c.   d.

3. Which sentence describes how two things are *similar*? Circle your answer.

   a. Fingers are longer than toes.
   b. Elbows and knees bend.
   c. Eyes can see and ears can hear.
   d. Hands can hold and feet can kick.

Name _____

Day 3 compare

1. **How would you complete this sentence? Say it aloud.**

   I can compare my friends by telling what they _____.

2. **How do you *compare* two things? Circle your answers.**

   a. Think about how they are alike.
   b. Think about how to make them better.
   c. Think about how to give them away.
   d. Think about how they are the same and how they are different.

3. **Which sentence *compares* two things? Circle your answer.**

   a. Snowflakes are made of water.
   b. Thunder can be very noisy.
   c. Snow is colder than rain.
   d. A tornado is a windstorm.

Day 4 comparison

1. **How would you complete this sentence? Say it aloud.**

   To make a comparison of two movies, I could tell about _____.

2. **Which sentence includes a *comparison*? Circle your answer.**

   a. Mountains and plains are both landforms.
   b. The Rocky Mountains are in North America.
   c. A plain is a large, flat area of land.
   d. Plains are good for farming.

3. **Which sentence uses *comparison* correctly? Circle your answer.**

   a. My poster will comparison snakes and fish.
   b. My poster shows a comparison of snakes and fish.
   c. We will comparison two poems about the sea.
   d. The comparison of water is land.

84 **WEEK 19** Daily Academic Vocabulary • EMC 2758 • © Evan-Moor Corporation

Name_____

Day 5 compare • comparison
different • similar

Daily Academic Vocabulary

Fill in the bubble next to the correct answer.

1. How are an ocean and a lake *different*?

- Ⓐ An ocean has salt water and a lake has fresh water.
- Ⓑ Both an ocean and a lake are bodies of water.
- Ⓒ You can measure how deep they both are.
- Ⓓ Both an ocean and a lake can be deeper after it rains.

2. What do two *similar* things always have?

- Ⓕ the same size
- Ⓖ different colors
- Ⓗ moving parts
- Ⓙ something that is the same

3. Which sentence *compares* two dogs?

- Ⓐ Loopy and Red run in the field.
- Ⓑ Red chases Loopy's tail.
- Ⓒ Loopy and Red like to play fetch.
- Ⓓ Red has longer hair than Loopy.

4. What does a *comparison* tell you?

- Ⓕ how something could be improved
- Ⓖ how two things are the same and not the same
- Ⓗ how two things should be saved to use again
- Ⓙ how something can be changed

Writing *Compare* two *different* kinds of pets. Tell one way they are *similar*. Tell one way they are *different*. Use the words *similar* and *different* in your writing.

_____

_____

_____

© Evan-Moor Corporation • EMC 2758 • Daily Academic Vocabulary   **WEEK 19**

Daily Academic Vocabulary

WEEK 20: place • replace • remove

Use the reproducible definitions on page 177 and the suggestions on page 6 to introduce the words for each day.

DAY 1

place
(noun) A specific area or location. *This is the perfect **place** for a picnic.*

Say: *I am going to describe a **place**. There are a lot of books there. They are in order. You can borrow them. What **place** am I describing?* (a library) Have students take turns describing mystery **places**. Encourage them to include both general **places** (e.g., playground; forest) and specific **places**. (e.g., Korea; Elm Street) Then conduct the first activity for Day 1 on page 87. Have students complete the Day 1 activities on their own, in pairs, or as a group.

DAY 2

place
(noun) Position or order. *I won a ribbon for coming in second **place**.*

Ask four students to stand up and form a line. Once in a line, ask each student: *What **place** are you in?* Have them respond with, "I am in ___ **place**." After they sit down, ask: *Has anyone ever been in a race or contest? What **place** did you come in?* Say: ***Place** can mean your position in something, like a line, or the order you came in.* Then conduct the first activity for Day 2 on page 87. Have students complete the Day 2 activities on their own, in pairs, or as a group.

DAY 3

place
(verb) To put in a specific spot or location. ***Place** the picnic basket on the table.*

replace
(verb) To put one thing or person in the place of another. *Dylan is ill, so Sarah will **replace** him as line leader.*

Choose two new or replacement books for your library corner/shelf. Hold up one book and ask: *Where can I **place** this book?* Repeat the question with various objects. Then show the new books and say: *Here are some new books for our library corner shelf. They will **replace** some books that are already there.* Give the books to a student and say: *Please take these books and **replace** two books that are already on the shelf. The new books will **replace** the old books.* Then conduct the first activity for Day 3 on page 88. Have students complete the Day 3 activities on their own, in pairs, or as a group.

DAY 4

remove
(verb) To take something off or away. *When we enter the classroom, we **remove** our jackets and hang them up.*

Say: *If I wanted to change the calendar to a new month, I would **remove** the name of this month and replace it with the name of the new month. What are some other items in the classroom that we might **remove** or take away?* Encourage students to use **remove** in their responses. Then conduct the first activity for Day 4 on page 88. Have students complete the Day 4 activities on their own, in pairs, or as a group.

DAY 5

Have students complete page 89. Call on students to read aloud their answers to the writing activity.

Name _____

Day 1 place

1. How would you complete this sentence? Say it aloud.

   My favorite place to read is _____.

2. Which of these are *places*? Circle your answers.

a.   b.   c.   d.

3. Which sentence does <u>not</u> use *place* correctly? Circle your answer.

   a. I put the place away in the closet.
   b. We went to a new place to eat.
   c. I'll save a place for you on the bus.
   d. I looked in each place, but I can't find my book.

Day 2 place

1. How would you complete this sentence? Say it aloud.

   If I came in first place in a contest, I would _____.

2. Which sentence uses *place* correctly? Circle your answer.

   a. I think my sister will first place in the race tomorrow.
   b. The runner third placed in yesterday's race.
   c. Jada finished the race in second place.
   d. You can try hard if you place.

3. What does it mean to have the second *place* in a line? Circle your answer.

   a. Two people are waiting by your side.
   b. You are the line leader.
   c. Two people started to run after you did.
   d. Only one person is ahead of you.

© Evan-Moor Corporation • EMC 2758 • Daily Academic Vocabulary   **WEEK 20**   87

Name_____

Day 3 place • replace

1. **How would you complete these sentences? Say them aloud.**

    When I get home, I place my schoolwork _____.

    I would like to replace my old _____ with a new one.

2. **If you *place* something on a table, what do you do with it? Circle your answer.**

    a. Put it on the table.
    b. Take it off the table.
    c. Clean the table with it.
    d. Break the table with it.

3. **Which sentence does not use *replace* correctly? Circle your answer.**

    a. We replace our pencils each month.
    b. I need to replace this old, worn-down one.
    c. It doesn't replace well anymore.
    d. I will replace my old jacket with a new one.

Day 4 remove

1. **How would you complete this sentence? Say it aloud.**

    If we remove all of the chairs from this classroom, _____.

2. **In which sentence does somebody *remove* something? Circle your answer.**

    a. Sonjay paints a picture of a mountain lion.
    b. Lisa fixes a mistake in her picture.
    c. Alan takes the red crayon out of the box.
    d. Myra adds three new tubes of paint to her paint set.

3. **What happens if you *remove* your shoes? Circle your answer.**

    a. You are not wearing them anymore.
    b. They are cleaner than they were before.
    c. You put them in your closet.
    d. They fit well and feel comfortable.

88 **WEEK 20** Daily Academic Vocabulary • EMC 2758 • © Evan-Moor Corporation

Name_____

Day 5 place • replace • remove

Fill in the bubble next to the correct answer.

1. Which of these sentences names a *place*?

- Ⓐ Tomika makes a new hat.
- Ⓑ Reg buys a stuffed animal.
- Ⓒ Anita runs very fast.
- Ⓓ Vinh goes to the store.

2. Which sentence tells someone's *place* in a spelling contest?

- Ⓕ Lola practiced for many hours.
- Ⓖ Lola's brother helped her learn new words.
- Ⓗ Lola felt nervous before the contest.
- Ⓙ Lola almost won, but she came in second.

3. Which of these is something you often *replace* in your home?

- Ⓐ the ceiling
- Ⓑ the bathtub
- Ⓒ a light bulb
- Ⓓ the front door

4. What happens when you *remove* a problem?

- Ⓕ You make the problem worse.
- Ⓖ You take away the problem.
- Ⓗ You think about the problem.
- Ⓙ You talk about the problem.

Writing   What is your favorite *place?* If you had to *remove* one thing from it, what would you *remove?* Use the words *place* and *remove* in your writing.

_____

_____

_____

© Evan-Moor Corporation • EMC 2758 • Daily Academic Vocabulary   **WEEK 20**

Daily Academic Vocabulary

WEEK 21: record • result

Use the reproducible definitions on page 178 and the suggestions on page 6 to introduce the words for each day.

DAY 1

record
(noun) Information or facts that are written down. *We kept a record of each day's weather.*

In preparation for the lesson, prepare or locate a chart that shows a **record** of something done in class. (e.g., results of a science experiment; notes on a topic) Say: *This is a record of something we did in class. What does it show?* (facts; information; what we learned) Then ask: *What other things might we make a record of?* Encourage students to respond by saying, "I might make a **record** of ___." (books I read; vocabulary words I learned) Conduct the first activity for Day 1 on page 91. Then have students complete the Day 1 activities on their own, in pairs, or as a group.

DAY 2

record
(verb) To write something down so that it can be kept. *We record the weather on our weather chart each day.*

Say: *I'd like to make a record of what we did in our classroom today (or yesterday). Tell me the things we did, and I will record (rē cord´) them on the board.* Then say: *Now it's your turn to record a list of words that I tell you.* Provide paper and pencils and ask students to write down three or four words they know how to spell. Say: *You recorded the words that I said. You wrote them down.* Then conduct the first activity for Day 2 on page 91. Have students complete the Day 2 activities on their own, in pairs, or as a group.

DAY 3

result
(noun) Something that happens because something else happens. *That muddy puddle is one result of yesterday's rain.*

Fold a piece of paper in half and then in half again. Point to one corner and ask: *What will be the result if I cut off this corner?* After students predict different **results**, cut off the corner and open the paper. Say: *I cut off one corner. What happened as a result?* Then conduct the first activity for Day 3 on page 92. Have students complete the Day 3 activities on their own, in pairs, or as a group.

DAY 4

result
(verb) To happen from a cause. *A stain can result from spilled juice.*

Ask: *What might result from an earthquake?* (damage to buildings; injuries to people) *What might result from a sunny day in winter?* (snow melts; people feel cheerful) *What can result from doing your homework?* Then conduct the first activity for Day 4 on page 92. Have students complete the Day 4 activities on their own, in pairs, or as a group.

DAY 5

Have students complete page 93. Call on students to read aloud their answers to the writing activity.

Name_____

Day 1 record

1. How would you complete this sentence? Say it aloud.

   It would be useful to keep a record of _____.

2. Which of the following are *records*? Circle your answers.

   a. a report card that shows a student's grades
   b. a signed photo of a basketball player
   c. a dream that takes place
   d. a chart that shows the weather last week

3. What does every *record* include? Circle your answer.

   a. stories   c. facts
   b. math problems   d. pictures

Day 2 record

1. How would you complete this sentence? Say it aloud.

   I can record how much I am growing by _____.

2. Which of these things can you use to *record* something? Circle your answers.

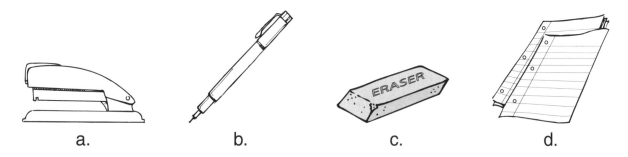

a.   b.   c.   d.

3. In which sentences do people *record* something? Circle your answers.

   a. Kyle sings his favorite song for his family.
   b. Hoon writes down how many games his team has won.
   c. Pam makes a list of books she has read.
   d. Cara goes swimming in the pond.

Name_____

Day 3 result

1. **How would you complete this sentence? Say it aloud.**

    If I read more books, the result will be _____.

2. **What makes something a *result*? Circle your answer.**

    a. It happens in the morning.
    b. It happens to somebody else.
    c. It happens because of something else.
    d. It happens for a long time.

3. **Which sentence uses *result* correctly? Circle your answer.**

    a. One result of exercise is a stronger body.
    b. We result when we run during recess.
    c. She won the race because she came in first result.
    d. He keeps a result of how many times he jumps.

Day 4 result

1. **How would you complete this sentence? Say it aloud.**

    Being tired can result from _____.

2. **Which sentence uses *result* correctly? Circle your answer.**

    a. My teeth result white when I brush them.
    b. The dentist results me to brush my teeth.
    c. I result my teeth because I want them to be clean.
    d. Clean teeth can result from daily brushing.

3. **Which of these can *result* from too much sun? Circle your answer.**

    a. rain   c. more books to read
    b. a sunburn   d. the moon

Name_____

Day 5   record • result

Fill in the bubble next to the correct answer.

1. In which sentence does someone make a *record* of something?
    - Ⓐ Lian walks from her home to school.
    - Ⓑ Lian keeps a chart of the birds she sees.
    - Ⓒ Lian writes a poem for her father's birthday.
    - Ⓓ Lian draws a picture for her father.

2. How can you *record* the events of a field trip?
    - Ⓕ Write down what you do.
    - Ⓖ Try to make the trip better.
    - Ⓗ Change the order of events.
    - Ⓙ Go on a trip with your friends.

3. Which sentence describes a *result*?
    - Ⓐ We watched a movie on TV last night.
    - Ⓑ My family eats dinner at six o'clock.
    - Ⓒ She goes to sleep because she is tired.
    - Ⓓ We painted the room a bright blue.

4. Which of these will most likely *result* in an accident?
    - Ⓕ Following all the safety rules at the pool.
    - Ⓖ Looking carefully before you cross the street.
    - Ⓗ Running without looking where you are going.
    - Ⓙ Washing and cleaning a cut on your finger.

My slim figure is the **result** of flying.

Writing   Think of an exciting event in your life. How could you keep a *record* of the event? What might happen as a *result* of the event? Use the words *record* and *result* in your writing.

_____

_____

_____

Daily Academic Vocabulary

WEEK 22

reply • report

Use the reproducible definitions on page 179 and the suggestions on page 6 to introduce the words for each day.

DAY 1

reply
(verb) To give or say an answer or response. *The teacher will reply to questions from the students.*

Point out that you can **reply** to a question. Say: *How would you reply to this question: What character from a book would you like to meet?* Explain that you can also **reply** to something someone says. Say: *Suppose someone says that libraries do not have books. How would you reply?* (disagree; libraries have books) Encourage students to use the word **reply** in their responses. Then conduct the first activity for Day 1 on page 95. Have students complete the Day 1 activities on their own, in pairs, or as a group.

DAY 2

reply
(noun) An answer or response. *Her reply to the question was clear and correct.*

Ask three students to name their favorite movie. Write the responses on the board. Follow up by asking the rest of the class: *How would your reply be different? Which replies name movies you have seen?* Point out that a **reply** can be written or spoken. Say: *When I ask you to name your favorite movie, your reply could be saying the title or writing it down.* Then conduct the first activity for Day 2 on page 95. Have students complete the Day 2 activities on their own, in pairs, or as a group.

DAY 3

report
(noun) A written or spoken description of something. *He is writing a report on different kinds of volcanoes.*

Ask: *Where could you find a report about something important that happened yesterday?* (newspaper; TV; Internet) *What information would a complete report about a famous person include?* (where born; why famous; where live) Ask: *Who would you like to give a report on? Why?* Encourage students to use the word **report** in their responses. Then conduct the first activity for Day 3 on page 96. Have students complete the Day 3 activities on their own, in pairs, or as a group.

DAY 4

report
(verb) To give a written or spoken description of something. *The student reports to his parents what he did in school.*

Ask one student to describe what he or she did over a school break. Then say: *(Student's name) just reported what he/she did over the break.* Then ask: *How could you report today's weather to someone who lives in another city?* (letter; e-mail; phone call) Then conduct the first activity for Day 4 on page 96. Have students complete the Day 4 activities on their own, in pairs, or as a group.

DAY 5

Have students complete page 97. Call on students to read aloud their answers to the writing activity.

Name_____

Day 1 reply

1. **How would you complete this sentence? Say it aloud.**

    If you ask me to name my favorite book, I will reply _____.

2. **In which sentences does someone *reply* to something? Circle your answers.**

    a. James trades baseball cards with Adam.

    b. Pilar adds another character to her story.

    c. Hoy answers his father's question.

    d. Clea says that she agrees with her brother.

3. **What can you use to *reply* to a question? Circle your answers.**

    a. a pen   c. your voice

    b. your feet   d. a TV

Day 2 reply

1. **How would you complete this sentence? Say it aloud.**

    If you ask me what I want to do tomorrow, my reply will be _____.

2. **Which of these are *replies*? Circle your answers.**

    a. a memory of a family dinner

    b. an answer to a question on a test

    c. learning to play the piano

    d. a response to someone's opinion

3. **In which sentence does someone give a *reply*? Circle your answer.**

    a. Loren uses a camera to take photos of her friends.

    b. Loren reads a book about making movies.

    c. Loren finds an old family photo in the attic.

    d. Loren writes a thank-you note for the present.

Name_____

Day 3 report

1. **How would you complete this sentence? Say it aloud.**

   For a science project, I could give a report about _____.

2. **What does a *report* always do? Circle your answer.**

   a. It makes something better.
   b. It changes something.
   c. It describes something.
   d. It gets rid of something.

3. **Which of these are *reports*? Circle your answers.**

   a. a rabbit that has long ears
   b. two friends who build a hamster cage
   c. a newspaper article about a state fair
   d. a student telling about how seeds become flowers

Day 4 report

1. **How would you complete this sentence? Say it aloud.**

   I could report on _____.

2. **What does Ruby do if she *reports* on a contest? Circle your answer.**

   a. She wins the contest.
   b. She judges the contest.
   c. She describes the contest.
   d. She tries to remember the contest.

3. **Which sentence uses *report* correctly? Circle your answer.**

   a. I report when I practice ice-skating in the winter.
   b. The newspaper reported on yesterday's storm.
   c. Our class reported the TV show.
   d. We are going to a beach report this summer.

Name_____

Day 5 reply • report

Fill in the bubble next to the correct answer.

1. What do you do when you *reply* to something?
   - Ⓐ make it better
   - Ⓑ ignore it
   - Ⓒ like it a lot
   - Ⓓ respond to it

2. Which sentence is true?
   - Ⓕ A reply is always true.
   - Ⓖ A reply is always false.
   - Ⓗ A reply can be written or said aloud.
   - Ⓙ A reply always includes an opinion.

3. Where are you most likely to find a *report*?
   - Ⓐ in a newspaper
   - Ⓑ hanging on a tree
   - Ⓒ in a comic book
   - Ⓓ in a swimming pool

4. What do you do if you *report* on bees?
   - Ⓕ describe bees
   - Ⓖ get stung by a bee
   - Ⓗ run away from bees
   - Ⓙ like bees

You should **report** on parrots!

Writing Think about giving a book *report* in front of the class. What book would you *report* on? Would you *reply* to questions from your audience? Use the words *report* and *reply* in your writing.

_____

_____

_____

Daily Academic Vocabulary

WEEK 23

know • knowledge

Use the reproducible definitions on page 180 and the suggestions on page 6 to introduce the words for each day.

DAY 1

know
(verb) To be certain about the facts or that something is true. *I **know** that a triangle has three corners and three sides.*

Ask each student to write down one thing he or she **knows** about shapes. Say: *Now you can share what you **know**.* Have students read their responses aloud. Ask: *Do you **know** the names of five different shapes?* Conduct the first activity for Day 1 on page 99. Then have students complete the Day 1 activities on their own, in pairs, or as a group.

DAY 2

know
(verb) To be familiar with a person, place, or thing. *My best friend and I **know** each other very well.*

Remind students that you can **know** a fact. Point out that you also can **know** a person, place, or thing. Ask: *What are some places you **know** that are very close to school? What people do you **know** who work at school but are not teachers?* Conduct the first activity for Day 2 on page 99. Then have students complete the Day 2 activities on their own, in pairs, or as a group.

DAY 3

know
(verb) To have skill in doing something. *Eduardo **knows** how to speak English and Spanish.*

Tie three pieces of string together. Ask: *Who **knows** how to make a braid?* Invite a volunteer who knows how to braid to demonstrate. Then ask: *Who **knows** how to tie a knot? Who **knows** how to measure the length of this string?* Say: *These are all skills that you **know**.* Ask: *What are other skills that you **know**? How do you **know** them?* Then conduct the first activity for Day 3 on page 100. Have students complete the Day 3 activities on their own, in pairs, or as a group.

DAY 4

knowledge
(noun) The things that one understands from having done them or studied them. *Her **knowledge** of soccer comes from playing the sport for many years.*

Ask: *What have we studied in class recently?* (telling time; magnets; writing sentences) Then say: *Because we have studied them, you now have **knowledge** of them. Your **knowledge** also includes things you have done. Raise your hand if you take piano lessons. Raise your hand if you play soccer. Raise your hand if you speak another language. You have **knowledge** of all these things. How could you increase your **knowledge**?* Finally, conduct the first activity for Day 4 on page 100. Have students complete the Day 4 activities on their own, in pairs, or as a group.

DAY 5

Have students complete page 101. Call on students to read aloud their answers to the writing activity.

Name _____

Day 1 know

1. How would you complete this sentence? Say it aloud.

   Something interesting I know about an animal is that _____.

2. Joni *knows* all the addition facts to 18. Which sentence is true? Circle your answer.

   a. Joni did a math paper with addition facts.
   b. Joni has memorized the addition facts to 18.
   c. Joni will learn the addition facts to 18 this year.
   d. Joni has addition facts flash cards.

3. Which sentences use *know* correctly? Circle your answers.

   a. Pedro and Lily know where the secret prize is hidden.
   b. Alana and her sister know before they go to school.
   c. Leslie knows the problem to make it go away.
   d. Toshiro knows the capital of France.

Day 2 know

1. How would you complete this sentence? Say it aloud.

   I know _____ because we live in the same neighborhood.

2. Oliver *knows* Mr. Hong. Which sentence is true? Circle your answer.

   a. Oliver does not like Mr. Hong.
   b. Oliver is afraid of Mr. Hong.
   c. Oliver wants to meet Mr. Hong.
   d. Oliver has met Mr. Hong.

3. Which sentence tells about someone who *knows* Chicago? Circle your answer.

   a. Chris is going to visit Chicago for the first time next year.
   b. Farida wants to visit Chicago because her cousin lives there.
   c. Shondra's grandmother has taken her many places in Chicago.
   d. Ike wrote a report on Chicago, even though he has never been there.

© Evan-Moor Corporation • EMC 2758 • Daily Academic Vocabulary   **WEEK 23**   99

Name_____

Daily Academic Vocabulary

Day 3 know

1. How would you complete this sentence? Say it aloud.

    I know how to _____.

2. Reggie *knows* how to walk home from school. Which sentence is true? Circle your answer.

    a. Reggie wants to learn how to walk home from school.
    b. Reggie thinks that walking home from school is a lot of fun.
    c. Reggie can walk home from school without getting lost.
    d. Reggie walks home from school with a friend.

3. Which sentence describes someone who *knows* something? Circle your answer.

    a. Helen can speak Japanese.
    b. Benito wants to take Japanese lessons.
    c. Dennis will visit Japan next year.
    d. Ida has a poster of Japan.

Day 4 knowledge

1. How would you complete this sentence? Say it aloud.

    My knowledge of _____ comes from _____.

2. Which sentence tells about someone's *knowledge*? Circle your answer.

    a. Jack's favorite food is peanut butter.
    b. Hama wants to read more about bugs.
    c. Gus had a dream about a big waterfall.
    d. Ramona understands a lot about farms.

3. Which sentence uses *knowledge* correctly? Circle your answer.

    a. Alice will knowledge to learn more about ballet.
    b. Alice knowledges a lot about sports.
    c. Alice got her knowledge of football from her uncle.
    d. Alice writes a knowledge about her favorite sport.

Name_____

Day 5   know • knowledge

Daily Academic Vocabulary

Fill in the bubble next to the correct answer.

1. Which sentence shows that Rita *knows* something?

    Ⓐ Rita picks flowers.
    Ⓑ Rita dreams about visiting a rainforest.
    Ⓒ Rita gives the correct answer on a test.
    Ⓓ Rita goes for a walk with her grandparents.

2. Victor *knows* Tej. Which sentence must be true?

    Ⓕ Victor has met Tej.
    Ⓖ Victor wants to meet Tej.
    Ⓗ Victor does not like Tej.
    Ⓙ Victor likes Tej.

3. Elena *knows* how to ride a bicycle. Which sentence must be true?

    Ⓐ Elena has a bicycle.
    Ⓑ Elena wants to learn how to ride a bicycle.
    Ⓒ Elena's favorite activity is riding her bicycle.
    Ⓓ Elena has the skills needed to ride a bicycle.

4. What is your *knowledge*?

    Ⓕ things you understand or know about
    Ⓖ things that you enjoy doing
    Ⓗ things that you want to learn
    Ⓙ things that other people know about you

Writing   Describe something you *know* how to do. How did you get this *knowledge?* Be sure to use the words *know* and *knowledge* in your writing.

_____

_____

_____

© Evan-Moor Corporation • EMC 2758 • Daily Academic Vocabulary   **WEEK 23**   101

Daily Academic Vocabulary

WEEK 24

believe • belief
clue • hint

Use the reproducible definitions on page 181 and the suggestions on page 6 to introduce the words for each day.

DAY 1

believe
(verb) To feel that something is true, real, or important. *I believe dogs are the best pets.*

Create a two-column chart. Write "know" in one column and "believe" in the other. Ask: *What are some things you know about cats?* (e.g., they are mammals; most of them have fur) *What are some things people believe about cats?* (e.g., black cats are bad luck; cats are smarter than dogs) Emphasize that when you **believe** something, your thinking is based on a feeling, not a fact. Then conduct the first activity for Day 1 on page 103. Have students complete the Day 1 activities on their own, in pairs, or as a group.

DAY 2

belief
(noun) Something that one feels is true or real. *It is his belief that soccer is the best sport.*

Say: *It is my belief that second grade is the best grade. I believe this is true. However, it is not a fact because it can't be proven.* Ask: *What is the difference between a belief and a fact?* (A fact can be proven; a **belief** is something you feel to be true.) Then ask: *What is a belief that you have about our school?* Finally, conduct the first activity for Day 2 on page 103. Have students complete the Day 2 activities on their own, in pairs, or as a group.

DAY 3

clue
(noun) A piece of information that helps one solve a problem or mystery. *Karen used the clues to solve the riddle.*

Ask a student to think of an object in the room. Say: *Give us one clue about the thing you are thinking about, but don't say exactly what it is.* Allow students to guess the secret object. Have the volunteer give additional **clues** if necessary. Discuss different kinds of **clues** students might give. (e.g., color; location) Then conduct the first activity for Day 3 on page 104. Have students complete the Day 3 activities on their own, in pairs, or as a group.

DAY 4

hint
(noun) A slight suggestion or helpful tip. *Please give me a hint to help me solve this math problem.*

(verb) To give a slight suggestion about something. *I will hint that I would like a game for my birthday.*

Say: *Suppose you know a first-grader who is learning to add. What hints can you give to make adding easier?* (e.g., draw a picture, use your fingers) *At what point might you hint about the correct answer to a problem?* (when someone is having a hard time solving it) Then ask: *When has someone given you hints about something? When have you hinted about something that you wanted?* Conduct the first activity for Day 4 on page 104. Have students complete the Day 4 activities on their own, in pairs, or as a group.

DAY 5

Have students complete page 105. Call on students to read aloud their answers to the writing activity.

Name _____

Day 1 believe

1. How would you complete this sentence? Say it aloud.

   I believe that school _____.

2. Which sentence describes someone who *believes* something? Circle your answer.

   a. Kia goes to the library to find out about whales.
   b. The librarian helps her find a useful book.
   c. Kia thinks that whales are the most interesting animals.
   d. Kia's brother reads the book.

3. Leslie *believes* that Frida is telling the truth. Which sentence is true? Circle your answer.

   a. Leslie does not trust Frida.
   b. Leslie thinks that Frida is being truthful.
   c. Leslie knows that Frida cannot be trusted.
   d. Leslie wants Frida to stop lying.

Day 2 belief

1. How would you complete this sentence? Say it aloud.

   It is my belief that students should _____.

2. Which sentence tells a *belief*? Circle your answer.

   a. Gardens are more important than parking lots.
   b. A rose is a flower with thorns.
   c. Trees are usually taller than bushes.
   d. Plants need water to stay alive.

3. Paul shares his *beliefs* about friendship. What does he do? Circle your answer.

   a. Paul tries to make new friends.
   b. Paul tells his friends about his trip.
   c. Paul explains how he feels about friends.
   d. Paul shares his new toys with his friends.

© Evan-Moor Corporation • EMC 2758 • Daily Academic Vocabulary   **WEEK 24**   103

Name_____

Daily Academic Vocabulary

Day 3 clue

1. How would you complete this sentence? Say it aloud.

A clue about when my birthday is would be _____.

2. Which sentences use *clue* correctly? Circle your answers.

a. The students clued to find the missing teacher.
b. They followed clues that the teacher left behind.
c. One important clue was a pen in the hall.
d. The students found the clue teacher in the gym.

3. In which sentence does someone give a *clue*? Circle your answer.

a. He tells the class that his name is Martin.
b. She tells the class that she is a police detective.
c. He tells the class that his name begins with an **E**.
d. She tells the class that they will visit a police station.

Day 4 hint

1. How would you complete these sentences? Say them aloud.

Sometimes, I need a hint to help me figure out _____.

To help someone guess my favorite food, I could hint that _____.

2. Which sentence uses *hint* correctly? Circle your answer.

a. The hint to a problem is the answer.
b. A hint can help you answer a riddle.
c. You can hint the answer if you think hard.
d. A hint is the same thing as an opinion.

3. Why might you *hint* about something? Circle your answers.

a. to let people know how you feel about something
b. to give people the exact answer
c. to give a suggestion about how to do something
d. to ask people for help to solve a problem

Name_____

Day 5 believe • belief • clue • hint

Fill in the bubble next to the correct answer.

1. If Juan *believes* in the tooth fairy, he thinks that she is _____.
- Ⓐ imaginary
- Ⓑ beautiful
- Ⓒ real
- Ⓓ powerful

2. What is a *belief* always based on?
- Ⓕ a fact
- Ⓖ a dream
- Ⓗ a feeling
- Ⓙ a story

3. What can a *clue* help you do?
- Ⓐ run a race
- Ⓑ eat a healthy meal
- Ⓒ take a bath
- Ⓓ solve a puzzle

4. What is a *hint*?
- Ⓕ an answer
- Ⓖ a suggestion
- Ⓗ a mystery
- Ⓙ a problem

Writing What do you *believe* next year will be like? What is one *clue* that makes you *believe* this? Be sure to use the words *believe* and *clue* in your writing.

_____

_____

_____

WEEK 24

Daily Academic Vocabulary

WEEK 25

direct • indirect
direction • directions

Use the reproducible definitions on page 182 and the suggestions on page 6 to introduce the words for each day.

DAY 1

direct
(verb) To tell which way to go or what to do. *The museum guard can **direct** you to the dinosaur room.*

Say: ***Direct** can mean to tell which way to go. Can you **direct** me to a place in this room without using the words right or left?* Allow volunteers to **direct** you. Then say: ***Direct** can also mean to tell what to do.* Ask: *Who might **direct** traffic?* (a police officer) *Who might **direct** students?* (a teacher; a principal) Conduct the first activity for Day 1 on page 107. Then have students complete the Day 1 activities on their own, in pairs, or as a group.

DAY 2

direct
(adj.) Going in a straight line. *He pitches the ball in a **direct** path to the batter.*

indirect
(adj.) Not in a straight line. *The bus route from my house to school is **indirect** because it winds all over town.*

Draw two houses on the board. Ask: *How can I draw a **direct** path between these two houses?* (Draw a straight line.) *How might I draw an **indirect** path?* (Any other line is **indirect**. Draw curving, zigzagging, or looping paths.) Then ask: *How can I take a **direct** path to the back of the room? How can I take an **indirect** path?* Have students **direct** your route. Then conduct the first activity for Day 2 on page 107. Have students complete the Day 2 activities on their own, in pairs, or as a group.

DAY 3

direction
(noun) The way that someone or something is moving or pointing. *The road sign showed the **direction** to New Town.*

Say: *Point with your arm in the **direction** of the window. Now stand up. Take one step in my **direction**. Now turn in the **direction** of the door.* Point out that the word **direction** is often used in the phrase "in the **direction** of." Then conduct the first activity for Day 3 on page 108. Have students complete the Day 3 activities on their own, in pairs, or as a group.

DAY 4

directions
(noun) Instructions on how to do something. *The **directions** told us how to put the tent together.*

Ask: *Where have you found **directions**?* (games, toys, books, tests) *Where might you find the **directions** on a test?* (at the beginning) *What do **directions** often have to help you know the order in which to do things?* (numbers) Follow up by asking: *Why do you need to be careful when following **directions**?* (So you don't make a mistake.) Say: *Tell about a time when you did not follow **directions**. What happened?* Then conduct the first activity for Day 4 on page 108. Have students complete the Day 4 activities on their own, in pairs, or as a group.

DAY 5

Have students complete page 109. Call on students to read aloud their answers to the writing activity.

Name_____

Day 1 direct

1. How would you complete this sentence? Say it aloud.

   If I direct someone to the library, I would say to _____.

2. In which sentences does someone *direct* someone else? Circle your answers.

   a. Patty lends Dana a sleeping bag.
   b. Boris tells his younger brother a story.
   c. Carla tells Matt how to get to the store.
   d. Richard explains to Nye how to build a birdhouse.

3. A museum guide *directs* you to the moon rock. What does the guide do? Circle your answer.

   a. Explains why the moon rock is important.
   b. Tells you to visit the room with the moon rock.
   c. Thinks that you are interested in the moon.
   d. Tells you how to get to the room with the moon rock.

Day 2 direct • indirect

1. How would you complete these sentences? Say them aloud.

   A direct path from my seat to the door is _____.

   An indirect path from my classroom to the bathroom is _____.

2. Which line shows a *direct* path? Circle your answer.

 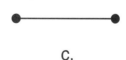 

   a.   b.   c.   d.

3. Which sentences are true? Circle your answers.

   a. A direct path is a straight line.
   b. Some direct paths turn in many directions.
   c. Indirect paths are not straight lines.
   d. An indirect path is always very short.

© Evan-Moor Corporation • EMC 2758 • Daily Academic Vocabulary   **WEEK 25**   107

Name _____

Day 3 | direction

1. How would you complete this sentence? Say it aloud.

    I went in the wrong direction when I _____.

2. Which sentence uses *direction* correctly? Circle your answer.

    a. The principal directions us to the parking lot.
    b. She gives me a direction to my question.
    c. We walked in the direction of the flagpole.
    d. We will direction to find our way back to class.

3. We drove in the *direction* of the ocean. Which sentence is true? Circle your answer.

    a. We drove toward the ocean.
    b. We drove underneath the ocean.
    c. We drove above the ocean.
    d. We drove away from the ocean.

Day 4 | directions

1. How would you complete this sentence? Say it aloud.

    I need to follow directions when I _____.

2. In which sentence does Joel read *directions*? Circle your answer.

    a. Joel reads a story about a boy building a car.
    b. Joel reads a poem about a car.
    c. Joel reads the instructions that came with his race car.
    d. Joel reads an article about a car race.

3. Where will you probably find *directions*? Circle your answers.

    a. with a game   c. on a pencil
    b. in a bucket   d. on a test

Always follow the **directions!**

108   **WEEK 25**   Daily Academic Vocabulary • EMC 2758 • © Evan-Moor Corporation

Name_____

Day 5 direct • indirect • direction • directions

Fill in the bubble next to the correct answer.

1. If someone *directs* you to the beach, what does this person do?

    Ⓐ drives you to the beach
    Ⓑ tells you how to get to the beach
    Ⓒ hints that you might enjoy the beach
    Ⓓ collects shells on the beach

2. On her way home, Janice follows a very *indirect* path. Which of these sentences is true?

    Ⓕ Janice follows a straight path home.
    Ⓖ Janice's path is very short.
    Ⓗ Janice's path is not a straight line.
    Ⓙ Janice's path is direct.

3. Soo Ha walks in the *direction* of the playground. What does she do?

    Ⓐ She walks toward the playground.
    Ⓑ She walks away from the playground.
    Ⓒ She walks around the playground.
    Ⓓ She walks out of the playground.

4. Which word means the same thing as *directions*?

    Ⓕ favorites
    Ⓖ instructions
    Ⓗ movements
    Ⓙ follows

Writing Tell about a time you did <u>not</u> follow *directions*. What happened? Be sure to use the word *directions* in your writing.

_____

_____

_____

Daily Academic Vocabulary

WEEK 26: pattern • copy • trace

Use the reproducible definitions on page 183 and the suggestions on page 6 to introduce the words for each day.

DAY 1

pattern
(noun) A repeating arrangement of colors, shapes, numbers, sounds, or other things. *The rhyming pattern of the poem made it easy to learn.*

Clap a **pattern**. Ask: *Can you repeat this clapping pattern?* Then draw these shapes on the board: circle, triangle, square, square, circle, triangle, square. Ask: *What shape comes next in this pattern?* (square) Have volunteers create **patterns** made up of shapes, numbers, or letters on the board. Then conduct the first activity for Day 1 on page 111. Have students complete the Day 1 activities on their own, in pairs, or as a group.

DAY 2

pattern
(noun) Actions or events that always happen in the same way or in the same order. *Our family's activities on Sunday always follow the same pattern.*

Ask: *Do you follow the same pattern every morning when you get ready for school?* (e.g., shower, breakfast, brush teeth) *When might you break your morning pattern?* (if you're late for school) *What patterns do we have in our school days or weeks?* Then conduct the first activity for Day 2 on page 111. Have students complete the Day 2 activities on their own, in pairs, or as a group.

DAY 3

copy
(noun) Something that looks or sounds exactly like another thing. *I have a copy of the famous painting <u>Sunflowers</u>.*

(verb) To write the exact words. *Please copy this sentence from the board.*

Draw a house on the board. Ask: *How can you make a copy of this house?* (e.g., draw the same shape on a piece of paper; take a photo; trace it) Then write on the board a familiar saying, such as "Time flies when you're having fun." Ask: *How can you copy this sentence?* (Write it down exactly.) Next, ask: *When might I ask you to copy a sentence? When would it be bad to copy something?* Then conduct the first activity for Day 3 on page 112. Have students complete the Day 3 activities on their own, in pairs, or as a group.

DAY 4

trace
(verb) To copy a picture or shape by following its outline. *We trace each letter before we write it.*

Show students a plate or other circular object. Ask: *What shape will I get if I trace this plate?* (circle) Demonstrate the result. Have students name the shapes that can be made by **tracing** other classroom objects. Then ask: *When have you traced something?* Finally, conduct the first activity for Day 4 on page 112. Have students complete the Day 4 activities on their own, in pairs, or as a group.

DAY 5

Have students complete page 113. Call on students to read aloud their answers to the writing activity.

Name _____

Daily Academic Vocabulary

Day 1 pattern

1. How would you complete this sentence? Say it aloud.

   I can figure out a pattern of numbers by _____.

2. What makes something a *pattern*? Circle your answer.

   a. It has circles in it.
   b. Something in it is very long.
   c. It has words in it.
   d. Something in it repeats.

3. Which sentence uses *pattern* correctly? Circle your answer.

   a. I pattern a dress by washing it.
   b. I use a pattern to remove the dirt from a necklace.
   c. The bracelet patterns green, yellow, and silver.
   d. I follow a pattern with beads when I make a bracelet.

Day 2 pattern

1. How would you complete this sentence? Say it aloud.

   The pattern of my school day starts with _____.

2. Which sentence shows a *pattern*? Circle your answer.

   a. On some nights, I stay up to read a book.
   b. Every night I take a bath, brush my teeth, and go to bed.
   c. Many nights I go to sleep at 8 p.m.
   d. Can I have a snack before I go to bed?

3. The events at a fair follow a *pattern.* Which sentence is true? Circle your answer.

   a. The events always happen in the same order.
   b. The events never happen in the same order.
   c. No one knows when the events will happen.
   d. The order of events will always be a surprise.

© Evan-Moor Corporation • EMC 2758 • Daily Academic Vocabulary   WEEK 26   111

Name_____

Day 3 copy

1. How would you complete these sentences? Say them aloud.

   If I like one of my drawings, I can make a copy by _____.

   I copy what the teacher writes when _____.

2. Which picture shows one thing and a *copy*? Circle your answer.

   Ee   EE   EF   eF
   a.   b.   c.   d.

3. If your teacher asks you to *copy* a word from the board, what should you do? Circle your answer.

   a. Think of a word that rhymes with the word on the board.
   b. Find another word that uses the same letters.
   c. Write the word exactly as it is on the board.
   d. Erase the word and write a new one in its place.

Day 4 trace

1. How would you complete this sentence? Say it aloud.

   If I want to draw a rectangle, I could trace a _____.

2. If you *trace* a leaf, which picture shows what you will get? Circle your answer.

a.   b.   c.   d.

3. In which sentence does Jae *trace* something? Circle your answer.

   a. Jae draws a picture of a giant monster.
   b. Jae stores his art supplies in a square box.
   c. Jae uses water to clean his paintbrushes.
   d. Jae draws a line around his foot with a marker.

Name_____

Day 5 pattern • copy • trace

Fill in the bubble next to the correct answer.

1. Which sentence describes a *pattern*?

    Ⓐ Her winter scarf is a deep red color.
    Ⓑ Her shirt has repeating red and white stripes.
    Ⓒ Her shoes are made of canvas and rubber.
    Ⓓ Her hair falls a little bit below her shoulders.

2. If you follow a *pattern* of events, what do you do?

    Ⓕ do different things each time
    Ⓖ go after something else
    Ⓗ do the same thing each time
    Ⓙ do what someone else says to do

3. Ken's poster is a *copy* of a famous painting. Which sentence is true?

    Ⓐ The poster looks exactly like the painting.
    Ⓑ The poster has different colors than the painting.
    Ⓒ The poster looks nothing like the painting.
    Ⓓ The poster was made before the painting.

4. What is one way you can you *trace* something?

    Ⓕ Roll it up and store it in a tube.
    Ⓖ Fold it and place it in an envelope.
    Ⓗ Follow its lines with a pencil.
    Ⓙ Tear it in half and throw away one part.

Writing Tell about a *pattern* that you follow in your life. What do you do? When do you do it? Be sure to use the word *pattern* in your writing.

_____

_____

_____

CUMULATIVE REVIEW
WORDS FROM WEEKS 19–26

belief
believe
clue
compare
comparison
copy
different
direct
direction
directions
hint
indirect
know
knowledge
pattern
place
record
remove
replace
reply
report
result
similar
trace

Days 1–4
Each day's activity is a cloze paragraph that students complete with words or forms of words that they have learned in weeks 19–26. Before students begin, pronounce each word in the box on the student page, have students repeat each word, and then review each word's meaning(s). **Other ways to review the words:**

- Start a sentence containing one of the words and have students finish the sentence orally. For example:

    *I might read the **directions** when I get a...*
    *I can **copy** a sentence by...*

- Provide students with a definition and ask them to supply the word that fits it.
- Ask questions that require students to know the meaning of each word. For example:

    *How might you increase your **knowledge** of Africa?*
    *How are a **direct** and an **indirect** path different?*
    *Why might you **remove** a hat?*

- Have students use each word in a sentence.

Day 5
Start by reviewing the words in the crossword activity for Day 5. Write the words on the board and have students repeat them after you. Provide a sentence for one of the words. Ask students to think of their own sentence and share it with a partner. Call on several students to share their sentences. Follow the same procedure for the remaining words. Then have students complete the crossword activity.

Extension Ideas
Use any of the following activities to help integrate the vocabulary words into other content areas:

- Ask students to **compare** two people who have made a difference in the world, such as Abraham Lincoln and Martin Luther King, Jr. Have students create a T-chart to list ways the people are **similar** and **different**.
- Have students create and display **patterns** by tracing geometric shapes. Then ask other students if they can continue the **patterns**.
- Have students predict the **results** of experiments with magnets. For example: What is the **result** of trying to pick up paper with a magnet? A paper clip? Then have them conduct experiments to test their **knowledge**.
- Have students read a school map to give **directions** for getting from one **place** to another. This could be used to teach fire drill procedures. Students can also use the map to give **clues** to a mystery location.

Name_____

Daily Academic Vocabulary

compare	directions	pattern	record	result
different	know	place	remove	

Day 1

Fill in the blanks with words from the word box.

How do you put up a tent? First, _____ all of the parts from the bag. Then, _____ the parts on the ground. Make sure you know the name of each part. Next, follow the _____ that came with the tent. Do each step carefully and the _____ will be a perfectly built tent. Once you _____ how to put the tent together, you will be able to do it more quickly the next time.

Day 2

Fill in the blanks with words from the word box.

A quilt is a blanket made of fabric pieces and scraps. The pieces often form a beautiful _____. You can _____ the shapes you see in quilts. Suppose you are looking at two _____ quilts. You might notice that one quilt is made of tiny squares and the other is made of triangles. You could count the shapes and keep a _____ of the number of each shape.

WEEK 27

Name _____

Daily Academic Vocabulary

| believe | direction | knowledge | similar |
| direct | indirect | reply | trace |

Day 3

Fill in the blanks with words from the word box.

Do you _____ that some things are lucky? Some people think that horseshoes, four-leaf clovers, or feathers will bring good luck. Other people have _____ feelings about different items. If you ask someone to name a lucky number, a common _____ might be seven. To make a good-luck poster, you might _____ the outline of a horseshoe.

Day 4

Fill in the blanks with words from the word box.

A compass can help you find a path. The needle on a compass always points in the _____ of north. The compass gives you the _____ you need to find your way. Of course, you may not be able to follow a _____ path to get where you're going. Something, like a tree or a mountain, might be in your way. Then, you will need to follow a path that is _____.

WEEK 27

Name_____

Day 5

Crossword Challenge

For each clue, write one of the words from the word box to complete the puzzle.

belief   comparison   different   knowledge   report
clues   copy   hint   replace

Across
1. opposite of *same*
3. something that looks like another
4. to put one thing in place of another
6. you follow these to solve a mystery
7. to give a slight suggestion
8. things you understand

Down
2. Jana wrote a book _____ on "Mice and Beans."
3. the act of judging how two things are alike or different
5. something that one feels is true or real

Daily Academic Vocabulary

WEEK 28

state • statement • restate

Use the reproducible definitions on page 184 and the suggestions on page 6 to introduce the words for each day.

DAY 1

state
(noun) The condition of a person or thing. *He was in a **state** of shock when his Earth Day poster won first place.*

Say: *Imagine that we never put anything away or cleaned up after ourselves in this classroom. What would the **state** of the room be after a week?* Rephrase student responses by saying, *The room would be in a messy (or dirty) **state**.* Then say: *What if I said to you, "You look like you're in a good **state** of mind today." How could you look that might cause me to say that?* (happy; calm; attentive) You may wish to introduce other common phrases, such as "**state** of health." Conduct the first activity for Day 1 on page 119. Then have students complete the Day 1 activities on their own, in pairs, or as a group.

DAY 2

state
(verb) To use words to say, tell, or explain. *Please **state** your name clearly so we can hear you.*

Call on students to respond to the following: ***State** your name. **State** your birthday. **State** one thing you'd like to learn.* Say: *When you **stated** the information, you said it.* Then conduct the first activity for Day 2 on page 119. Then have students complete the Day 2 activities on their own, in pairs, or as a group.

DAY 3

statement
(noun) Something that is put into words. *I agree with everything she said in her **statement**.*

Say: *I think that pigs are the smartest animal. Who agrees with my **statement**? Who disagrees with the **statement**?* Then have students make their own **statements** about animals. Point out that a **statement** can be true or false. For example, say: *I think pigs can fly.* Conduct the first activity for Day 3 on page 120. Then have students complete the Day 3 activities on their own, in pairs, or as a group.

DAY 4

restate
(verb) To say again in a new way or to repeat. *The judge will **restate** the law in simpler words to help us understand it.*

Say: ***Restate** can mean to say something using different words.* Write this sentence on the board: "Islands are landforms surrounded by water." Ask: *How could you **restate** this sentence?* (An island is land with water on all sides.) Say: *You told me what an island is, but you used different words.* Then say: ***Restate** can also mean to repeat something. Sometimes I **restate** the same words to make sure you heard what I said and to help you remember. Why might you want to **restate** something?* Then conduct the first activity for Day 4 on page 120. Then have students complete the Day 4 activities on their own, in pairs, or as a group.

DAY 5

Have students complete page 121. Call on students to read aloud their answers to the writing activity.

Name_____

Day 1 state

1. **How would you complete this sentence? Say it aloud.**

   I will stay in a good state of health if I _____.

2. **Which words might describe the *state* of a plant that has not been watered for a month? Circle your answers.**

   a. droopy   c. healthy
   b. green   d. brown

3. **Which sentence uses *state* correctly? Circle your answer.**

   a. Mel uses a state to help clean the park.
   b. Mel's mother asks him to state the park.
   c. Mel's state is cleaning the park tomorrow.
   d. After the cleanup, we were proud of the state of our park.

Day 2 state

1. **How would you complete this sentence? Say it aloud.**

   If someone asks what is my favorite subject, I would state _____.

2. **Oscar *states* that he likes ice-skating. Which word means the same as *states*? Circle your answer.**

   a. wonders   c. thinks
   b. hopes   d. says

3. **In which sentence does somebody *state* something? Circle your answer.**

   a. Billy plays in the park with his dog.
   b. Garth learns a new song on the piano.
   c. Ryan writes a poem for his father.
   d. Felicia tells the teacher her answer.

© Evan-Moor Corporation • EMC 2758 • Daily Academic Vocabulary **WEEK 28** 119

Name_____

Day 3 statement

1. **How would you complete this sentence? Say it aloud.**

   I agree with my teacher's statement that _____.

2. **In which sentence does somebody make a *statement*? Circle your answer.**

   a. Jane says that roller coasters are fun.
   b. Jane rides a roller coaster.
   c. Jane is afraid of roller coasters.
   d. Jane wants to ride a roller coaster.

3. **How do you make a *statement*? Circle your answer.**

   a. You read a letter.
   b. You remember something.
   c. You put something into words.
   d. You carry something to another place.

Day 4 restate

1. **How would you complete this sentence? Say it aloud.**

   My teacher might ask me to restate my answer because _____.

2. **What do you do when you *restate* something? Circle your answer.**

   a. Put it into new words.   c. Try to find an answer to it.
   b. Change what it means.   d. Turn it off.

3. **A famous saying is, "The more the merrier." Which sentence *restates* the saying? Circle your answer.**

   a. People are happy when they have good food.
   b. Things are more fun with more people.
   c. If you are sad, people around you will be sad.
   d. Good friends are more important than family.

Name_____

Day 5 state • statement • restate

Fill in the bubble next to the correct answer.

1. The garden is in its most beautiful *state* right now. Which sentence is true?
    - Ⓐ The garden is more than ten years old.
    - Ⓑ The condition of the garden is excellent.
    - Ⓒ The garden is filled with weeds.
    - Ⓓ One part of the garden is neater than the rest.

2. If you *state* the answer to a question, what do you do?
    - Ⓕ Think about it.
    - Ⓖ Say it out loud.
    - Ⓗ Forget it.
    - Ⓙ Give somebody a hint.

3. Which sentence uses *statement* correctly?
    - Ⓐ The twins statement when they do their homework.
    - Ⓑ Adding and subtracting are two kinds of statements.
    - Ⓒ Annie agrees with Vic's statement about homework.
    - Ⓓ The statement of my homework is finished.

4. In which sentence does somebody *restate* something?
    - Ⓕ Ida asks Martin for directions to the bake sale.
    - Ⓖ Martin tells Ida how to get there.
    - Ⓗ Ida says the directions in her own words.
    - Ⓙ Ida and Martin go to the bake sale and buy muffins.

Writing *Restate* this sentence: "Many hands make light work." What does this *statement* mean to you? Use one of this week's words in your writing.

_____

_____

_____

Daily Academic Vocabulary

WEEK 29: plan • prepare

Use the reproducible definitions on page 185 and the suggestions on page 6 to introduce the words for each day.

DAY 1

plan
(noun) An idea worked out ahead of time about how to do something. *Our **plan** is to go on a hike tomorrow.*

(verb) To work out ahead of time how to do something. *We **plan** how we will decorate for the party.*

Explain that a **plan** can help you do something that has many steps. Ask: *Do you need to follow a **plan** to eat lunch?* (No.) *Would a **plan** help you build a model volcano?* (Yes.) *What other activities might use a **plan**?* (e.g., other projects; anything with many steps) *What **plans** have you followed? How can you **plan** what you will do tomorrow?* (You can make a schedule.) Conduct the first activity for Day 1 on page 123. Then have students complete the Day 1 activities on their own, in pairs, or as a group.

DAY 2

plan
(verb) To mean to do something. *I **plan** to read the last chapter of my book tonight.*

Show students a calendar or planner. Ask: *What do you **plan** to do tomorrow? What do you **plan** to do this weekend? How can a calendar help you keep track of what you **plan** to do? Do you always do everything you **plan** to do?* Conduct the first activity for Day 2 on page 123. Then have students complete the Day 2 activities on their own, in pairs, or as a group.

DAY 3

prepare
(verb) To make or get yourself ready. *We **prepare** for the party by making our costumes.*

Write these subjects on the board: "spelling," "math," "reading." Ask: *How do you **prepare** for a test in each of these subjects?* (e.g., study spelling lists; practice math skills; reread a story) *How might you **prepare** for a visit to a cave?* (Read about caves; bring a sweater and camera.) Say: *When you are **prepared**, you are ready.* Ask: *Do you feel **prepared** for next year? Why or why not? What could help you feel **prepared**?* Conduct the first activity for Day 3 on page 124. Then have students complete the Day 3 activities on their own, in pairs, or as a group.

DAY 4

prepare
(verb) To put parts or ingredients together to make something. *Mara can **prepare** breakfast for herself and her brother.*

Write these foods on the board: "breakfast cereal," "trail mix," "peanut butter sandwich." Ask: *Do you know how to **prepare** one of these foods?* (Allow students to suggest how to **prepare** each food.) *Do you think there is more than one way to **prepare** a peanut butter sandwich?* (Yes, there are many different ways.) *What is your favorite sandwich to **prepare**?* Conduct the first activity for Day 4 on page 124. Then have students complete the Day 4 activities on their own, in pairs, or as a group.

DAY 5

Have students complete page 125. Call on students to read aloud their answers to the writing activity.

Name_____

Day 1 plan

1. **How would you complete these sentences? Say them aloud.**

    I made a plan when I _____.

    If I wanted to plan a party, I would _____.

2. **What does a *plan* tell you? Circle your answer.**

    a. why something is not real
    b. where you can find something
    c. why something is a mystery
    d. how to do something

3. **Rami *plans* his summer vacation. Which sentence is true? Circle your answer.**

    a. Rami works out what he will do during his summer vacation.
    b. Rami does not want to think about his summer vacation.
    c. Rami forgets about his summer vacation.
    d. Rami thinks that the winter is more important.

Day 2 plan

1. **How would you complete this sentence? Say it aloud.**

    This Saturday, I plan to _____.

2. **In which sentence does someone *plan* to do something? Circle your answer.**

    a. Lola means to visit her aunt next month.
    b. Sam writes an e-mail to his cousin.
    c. Betsy reads a book to her sister.
    d. Maya teaches Gia how to add and subtract.

3. **Which sentence uses *plan* correctly? Circle your answer.**

    a. Please plan me your favorite color.
    b. I feel plan when I want to do something.
    c. We plan to visit the Grand Canyon next year.
    d. I will plan your secret by following the clues.

© Evan-Moor Corporation • EMC 2758 • Daily Academic Vocabulary   **WEEK 29**   123

Name_____

Day 3 prepare

1. How would you complete this sentence? Say it aloud.

    I would prepare for a day at the beach by _____.

2. Jan *prepares* to go sledding. Which sentence has the same meaning? Circle your answer.

    a. Jan loves to go sledding.
    b. Jan gets ready to go sledding.
    c. Jan never goes sledding.
    d. Jan teaches sledding classes.

3. In which sentence is Marco *prepared*? Circle your answer.

    a. Marco knows that the White House is in Washington, D.C.
    b. Marco has an uncle who lives near the White House.
    c. Marco packed his suitcase for his trip.
    d. Marco can't wait to see his uncle.

Day 4 prepare

1. How would you complete this sentence? Say it aloud.

    If I want to make a special treat, I prepare a _____.

2. Which of the following things can you use to *prepare* soup? Circle your answers.

   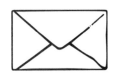 

a. b. c. d.

3. In which sentence does Lourdes *prepare* something? Circle your answer.

    a. Lourdes wants to find out how plants grow.
    b. Lourdes puts together her project for the science fair.
    c. Lourdes explains her project to the judges.
    d. Lourdes wins first place.

Name_____

Day 5 plan • prepare

Fill in the bubble next to the correct answer.

1. In which sentence does Tommy *plan* something?
    - Ⓐ Tommy wants to build a treehouse in his yard.
    - Ⓑ Tommy works out how he will put the house together.
    - Ⓒ Tommy dreams about dancing trees.
    - Ⓓ Tommy forgets how much wood he will need for the project.

2. Susie *plans* to go to the zoo. Which sentence has the same meaning?
    - Ⓕ Susie is afraid to go to the zoo.
    - Ⓖ Susie is not allowed to go to the zoo.
    - Ⓗ Susie means to go to the zoo soon.
    - Ⓙ Susie makes believe that she is at the zoo.

3. What do you do if you *prepare* to do something?
    - Ⓐ Try not to do it.
    - Ⓑ Get ready to do it.
    - Ⓒ Find a way to do something else instead.
    - Ⓓ Forget to do it.

4. How can you *prepare* a speech?
    - Ⓕ Put together what you will say.
    - Ⓖ Ask someone what to say.
    - Ⓗ Tell someone what to do.
    - Ⓙ Read a book of speeches.

Writing   What is something exciting you *plan* to do next month? How can you *prepare*? Use the words *plan* and *prepare* in your writing.

_____

_____

_____

Daily Academic Vocabulary

WEEK 30

observe • observation

Use the reproducible definitions on page 186 and the suggestions on page 6 to introduce the words for each day.

DAY 1

observe
(verb) To watch someone or something closely. *The owls **observe** the mice on the ground.*

Ask: *Where can you **observe** animals that are not pets?* (e.g., zoos, farms, nature programs) *What tools might help you **observe** wild animals?* (e.g., binoculars; cameras; notebooks) *What is the difference between playing with a cat and **observing** a cat?* (When you **observe**, you watch it carefully.) Conduct the first activity for Day 1 on page 127. Then have students complete the Day 1 activities on their own, in pairs, or as a group.

DAY 2

observation
(noun) The careful watching of something. *Our **observation** of the seed sprouting helped us understand how plants grow.*

Point out that science experiments often require close **observation**. Ask: *Why do you think **observation** is an important part of science?* (We have to look carefully at our world to understand how things work.) *Can you explain any **observations** you have made at school or elsewhere? Have you watched or examined something closely? What was it?* Conduct the first activity for Day 2 on page 127. Then have students complete the Day 2 activities on their own, in pairs, or as a group.

DAY 3

observe
(verb) To notice something by looking or watching. *As I look around the playground, I **observe** two girls jumping rope.*

Fill a glass of water about halfway. Mark the water level with a marking pen. Say: ***Observe** what happens to the water level when I add a marble (or another object) to the water. What do you **observe**?* (The water level rises.) ***Observe** what happens when I add more marbles.* Then conduct the first activity for Day 3 on page 128. Have students complete the Day 3 activities on their own, in pairs, or as a group.

DAY 4

observation
(noun) Something that is noticed or seen. *Please share your **observations** of the ants.*

Ask: *What **observation** might you make about what has happened in our classroom today?* Write down student **observations**. Emphasize that each **observation** is based on something that a student noticed or saw. Ask: *Why might two people make different **observations** about the same topic?* (They noticed or saw different things.) Conduct the first activity for Day 4 on page 128. Then have students complete the Day 4 activities on their own, in pairs, or as a group.

DAY 5

Have students complete page 129. Call on students to read aloud their answers to the writing activity.

Name_____

Day 1 observe

1. How would you complete this sentence? Say it aloud.

   Something I observe at school is _____.

2. In which sentence does Casey *observe* something? Circle your answer.

   a. Casey writes a report about ants.
   b. Casey draws a picture of an ant.
   c. Casey watches ants carrying sugar.
   d. Casey reads an article about ants.

3. How can you *observe* the moon? Circle your answer.

   a. Look at it closely with a telescope.
   b. Write a poem about it.
   c. Close your eyes and imagine what it looks like.
   d. Make a list of words that rhyme with "moon."

Day 2 observation

1. How would you complete this sentence? Say it aloud.

   I once made an observation of _____.

2. Tamyra carries out an *observation* of rain. What does she do? Circle your answer.

   a. watches rain very carefully
   b. goes inside when it begins to rain
   c. learns how to stop rain
   d. causes rain to begin falling

3. Which sentence uses *observation* correctly? Circle your answer.

   a. We observation the pattern of the clouds.
   b. After the snow, the ice begins to observation.
   c. I think the observation of weather is interesting.
   d. People use clues to observation the weather.

© Evan-Moor Corporation • EMC 2758 • Daily Academic Vocabulary   WEEK 30   127

Name_____

Day 3 observe

1. How would you complete this sentence? Say it aloud.

   When I look at this room, one of the first things I observe is _____.

2. Tracey *observes* the level of cereal in the box. What does she do? Circle your answer.

   a. She notices how much cereal is in the box.
   b. She adds more cereal to the box.
   c. She takes some cereal out of the box.
   d. She forgets how much cereal is in the box.

3. Which sentence means that you *observe* a crack in a glass? Circle your answer.

   a. You drop a glass by accident.
   b. You fix a glass that was broken.
   c. You see that a glass has a crack.
   d. You hope that the glass is not broken.

Day 4 observation

1. How would you complete this sentence? Say it aloud.

   It is my observation that a lot of TV shows are _____.

2. If you make an *observation,* what do you do? Circle your answer.

   a. Change something.   c. Fix something.
   b. Notice something.   d. Solve something.

3. In which sentence does someone make an *observation*? Circle your answer.

   a. Jack brings a new keyboard into the computer lab.
   b. Dana learns how to type using a computer keyboard.
   c. Van shuts down the computer before he leaves the room.
   d. Adam sees that one of the computer mouse pads is missing.

128 **WEEK 30**   Daily Academic Vocabulary • EMC 2758 • © Evan-Moor Corporation

Name_____

Day 5 observe • observation

Daily Academic Vocabulary

Fill in the bubble next to the correct answer.

1. If you *observe* a plant, what do you do?
    - Ⓐ Water it.
    - Ⓑ Take it out of the ground.
    - Ⓒ Watch it grow.
    - Ⓓ Put it in a bucket.

2. In which sentence does Harlan carry out an *observation*?
    - Ⓕ Harlan climbs to the top of a hill.
    - Ⓖ Harlan prepares a snack.
    - Ⓗ Harlan knows how to read a map.
    - Ⓙ Harlan carefully watches the fish in the tank.

3. Mona *observes* a new student at school. Which sentence has the same meaning?
    - Ⓐ Mona helps a new student.
    - Ⓑ Mona notices a new student.
    - Ⓒ Mona hides a new student.
    - Ⓓ Mona welcomes a new student.

4. Which statement is an *observation*?
    - Ⓕ I believe that it will rain tomorrow.
    - Ⓖ I notice that people are using umbrellas.
    - Ⓗ I would love to see a rainbow.
    - Ⓙ The weather will get better.

Writing   Think of an animal you would like to *observe*. What would you like to learn from your *observation*? Be sure to use the words *observe* and *observation* in your writing.

_____

_____

Daily Academic Vocabulary

WEEK 31

position • locate
located • location

Use the reproducible definitions on page 187 and the suggestions on page 6 to introduce the words for each day.

DAY 1

position
(noun) The place where someone or something is. *Please move those books to a new **position** so they are not in the way.*

Instruct students to place an object (e.g., pencil; book) on top of their desks. Say: *Change the **position** of the object. What did you do?* (moved it to a new place) Then write "9, 3, 5, 8, 1" on the board. Ask students to name the numeral that is in a specific **position**. For example, *What numeral is in the second **position**? What numeral is in the first **position** to the right of 5? What is the **position** of something?* (the place where it is) Conduct the first activity for Day 1 on page 131. Then have students complete the Day 1 activities on their own, in pairs, or as a group.

DAY 2

locate
(verb) To find out where something or someone is. *Will you help the new student **locate** the library?*

Show students a simple map. Ask: *What can you **locate** on this map?* Have students **locate** something on the map and tell the class, "I can **locate** ___." Then ask: *How might you **locate** something that you lost?* Conduct the first activity for Day 2 on page 131. Then have students complete the Day 2 activities on their own, in pairs, or as a group.

DAY 3

located
(verb) To be placed or found in a certain spot. *Rome is **located** in Italy.*

Ask: *Where is our school **located**?* (Answers include the street, neighborhood, city, state, country, continent, and planet.) *What things in this room are **located** in a corner? What things are **located** on a wall?* Give students hints of mystery objects in the room. Say: *The mystery object is **located** ___.* Then conduct the first activity for Day 3 on page 132. Have students complete the Day 3 activities on their own, in pairs, or as a group.

DAY 4

location
(noun) The place or position where something is. *The school office is in a nearby **location**.*

Tell students that you are going to name an object in the classroom and that they are going to describe the object's **location** by saying, "The **location** of ___ is ___." (on the bookshelf; in the closet; etc.) Name several objects and allow students to respond. Then ask: *What is your **location** in the room? How can you change your **location**?* Conduct the first activity for Day 4 on page 132. Then have students complete the Day 4 activities on their own, in pairs, or as a group.

DAY 5

Have students complete page 133. Call on students to read aloud their answers to the writing activity.

Name _____

Daily Academic Vocabulary

Day 1   position

1. How would you complete this sentence? Say it aloud.

    If I could change the position of my desk, I would _____.

2. I can't see the TV screen from this *position*.
   What is the best thing to do? Circle your answer.

    a. move my chair

    b. get a bigger TV

    c. tell the teacher to move the TV

    d. stand on my chair

3. Which sentence tells the *position* of a ruler? Circle your answer.

    a. The ruler is 15 centimeters long.

    b. The ruler is made of wood.

    c. The ruler is on the desk.

    d. The ruler is slightly bent.

Day 2   locate

1. How would you complete this sentence? Say it aloud.

    If one of my books is missing, I would try to locate it by first _____.

2. What does it mean to *locate* a city on a map?
   Circle your answer.

    a. Draw the city on the map.   c. Name the city on the map.

    b. Erase the city from the map.   d. Find the city on the map.

3. In which sentence does Lashanda *locate* something?
   Circle your answer.

    a. Lashanda reads a story about mountain climbing.

    b. Lashanda wonders what it would be like to climb a mountain.

    c. Lashanda figures out where Mount St. Helens is.

    d. Lashanda draws a mountain in a letter to her grandmother.

© Evan-Moor Corporation • EMC 2758 • Daily Academic Vocabulary   **WEEK 31**   131

Name_____

Daily Academic Vocabulary

Day 3 located

1. How would you complete this sentence? Say it aloud.

   My home is located _____.

2. Paris is *located* in France. Which sentence has the same meaning? Circle your answer.

   a. Paris is the capital of France.
   b. Paris is next to France.
   c. Paris is in France.
   d. Paris is near to France.

3. Which sentence tells you where a store is *located*? Circle your answer.

   a. The store sells food.
   b. The store is on Webber Street.
   c. The store is very large.
   d. The store has been there a long time.

Day 4 location

1. How would you complete this sentence? Say it aloud.

   I think the best location for riding a bike is _____.

2. If you know the *location* of a building, what do you know? Circle your answer.

   a. how old the building is
   b. how the building got its name
   c. what the building is made of
   d. where the building is

3. Which sentence uses *location* correctly? Circle your answer.

   a. The location of the treasure is a secret.
   b. We location the clues under rocks.
   c. Everyone locations one of the clues.
   d. It is my location that hunting for treasure is fun.

Name_____

Day 5 position • locate • located • location

Fill in the bubble next to the correct answer.

1. Alice changes the *position* of her bed. What does she do?
    - Ⓐ moves the bed to a new place
    - Ⓑ puts on clean sheets
    - Ⓒ buys a new bed
    - Ⓓ sells the bed

2. If you *locate* a book, what do you do?
    - Ⓕ write the book
    - Ⓖ read the book
    - Ⓗ find the book
    - Ⓙ hide the book

3. What might be *located* on a wall?
    - Ⓐ a building
    - Ⓑ a bridge
    - Ⓒ a window
    - Ⓓ a river

4. Which sentence tells the *location* of Mars?
    - Ⓕ Mars is a planet.
    - Ⓖ Mars is the fourth planet from the sun.
    - Ⓗ Mars is known for its red color.
    - Ⓙ Mars has been visited by an unmanned rover.

Writing Imagine you are going to build the perfect treehouse. How will you decide on the *location*? Where will you *locate* the materials you need? Use one of this week's words in your writing.

_____
_____
_____

Daily Academic Vocabulary

WEEK 32

complete • completely • completion

Use the reproducible definitions on page 188 and the suggestions on page 6 to introduce the words for each day.

DAY 1

complete
(adj.) Having all the needed parts; whole. *I found the missing piece, so the puzzle is complete again.*

completely
(adv.) Totally. *She filled in the form completely, making sure there were no blank spaces left.*

Write these letters on the board: "A," "E," "O." Ask: *Is this set of vowels complete?* (No.) *What letters should I add to make a complete set?* ("I" and "U") *If you make a set of alphabet cards with one card for each letter, how many cards will be in the complete set?* (26) *How will you know when you have completely finished the cards?* (when all 26 cards are done) *What do you think it means to completely finish a task?* (e.g., do all of it; leave nothing undone) *Why is that important?* Conduct the first activity for Day 1 on page 135. Then have students complete the Day 1 activities on their own, in pairs, or as a group.

DAY 2

complete
(verb) To finish or end. *Tonight I will complete the book I have been reading.*

Ask: *What does it mean to complete an assignment? Why is it important to complete something?* Then ask: *What other things are important to complete? What have you recently completed?* Encourage students to use the word **complete** in their responses. Conduct the first activity for Day 2 on page 135. Then have students complete the Day 2 activities on their own, in pairs, or as a group.

DAY 3

complete
(verb) To add what is missing. *We can complete the sentence by adding the missing verb.*

Write this sentence on the board: "The rocket ___ the moon." Ask: *How can you complete this sentence?* (e.g., goes to; flies past; lands on) Students can offer other sentences with missing parts and volunteers can **complete** them. Say: *Suppose someone is telling a story and stops in the middle. What would you do to complete the story?* (Tell the rest of the story; tell the ending.) Then conduct the first activity for Day 3 on page 136. Have students complete the Day 3 activities on their own, in pairs, or as a group.

DAY 4

completion
(noun) The act of bringing something to a finish or end. *An awards assembly will celebrate the completion of our school year.*

Ask: *If I say, "The completion of this project will take 3 days," what do I mean?* (It will take 3 days to complete.) *If I say, "The completion of the project depends on your cooperation," what do I mean?* Then ask: *What marks the completion of a school day? A school year? A phone call?* Then conduct the first activity for Day 4 on page 136. Have students complete the Day 4 activities on their own, in pairs, or as a group.

DAY 5

Have students complete page 137. Call on students to read aloud their answers to the writing activity.

Name _____

Day 1 complete • completely

1. How would you complete these sentences? Say them aloud.

   I know something is complete when _____.

   When my homework is completely finished, I _____.

2. Fiona has a *complete* deck of playing cards. What does she have? Circle your answer.

   a. very old playing cards
   b. one very special playing card
   c. all of the cards in one deck
   d. playing cards from other countries

3. In which sentence does somebody do something *completely*? Circle your answer.

   a. Kim puts together an entire model train.
   b. Ryan begins to make a toy airplane.
   c. Quy gets ready to play the piano.
   d. Brenda plans to study the violin.

Day 2 complete

1. How would you complete this sentence? Say it aloud.

   Before the end of this year, I would like to complete _____.

2. If you *complete* a project, what do you do? Circle your answer.

   a. Start working on the project.
   b. Prepare to work on the project.
   c. Plan how you will do the project.
   d. Finish the project.

3. Which sentence uses *complete* correctly? Circle your answer.

   a. The poet makes a complete to share with the class.
   b. The writer completes a poem and reads it aloud.
   c. We will complete in a writing contest this year.
   d. I always try to complete the mistakes in my writing.

© Evan-Moor Corporation • EMC 2758 • Daily Academic Vocabulary   **WEEK 32**   135

Name _____

Day 3 complete

1. How would you complete this sentence? Say it aloud.

   I can complete a letter to someone by _____.

2. Which numbers *complete* this set? Circle your answer.

   0, 1, 2, 3, __, 5, 6, __, 8, 9

   a. 6, 7   c. 2, 4
   b. 4, 7   d. 8, 9

3. If directions ask you to *complete* a picture, what should you do? Circle your answer.

   a. Erase the parts of the picture that you do not like.
   b. Add the parts of the picture that are missing.
   c. Change the parts of the picture that are wrong.
   d. Draw a new picture that is a copy.

Day 4 completion

1. How would you complete this sentence? Say it aloud.

   After the completion of this school year, I plan to _____.

2. Which one describes the *completion* of a puzzle? Circle your answer.

   a. sorting all the corner and edge pieces
   b. discovering that one of the pieces is missing
   c. finding all the pieces to the puzzle
   d. putting all the puzzle pieces together

3. Which sentence describes the *completion* of something? Circle your answer.

   a. We finish our garden project with a vegetable party.
   b. We decide that we will plant green beans next year.
   c. We draw plans that show where the plants will go.
   d. We hope that the vegetables will grow quickly.

136 WEEK 32   Daily Academic Vocabulary • EMC 2758 • © Evan-Moor Corporation

Name_____

Day 5 complete • completely • completion

Daily Academic Vocabulary

Fill in the bubble next to the correct answer.

1. If a game is *complete,* what does it have?
    - Ⓐ only one missing part
    - Ⓑ more than one missing part
    - Ⓒ all of its parts
    - Ⓓ no parts at all

Parrots are _____.

2. In which sentence does Rani *complete* something?
    - Ⓕ Rani finishes making a movie.
    - Ⓖ Rani begins to draw a picture.
    - Ⓗ Rani plans a photo album.
    - Ⓙ Rani hurries to the camera store.

3. How can you *complete* a sentence?
    - Ⓐ Copy the sentence exactly.
    - Ⓑ Write a new sentence that rhymes.
    - Ⓒ Think of another sentence on the same topic.
    - Ⓓ Add the missing words.

4. Which one describes the *completion* of a form?
    - Ⓕ filling in all the information
    - Ⓖ asking questions about the form
    - Ⓗ changing the information on the form
    - Ⓙ throwing away the form

Writing Think of a new project you would like to begin. What do you need to do to *complete* it? How will you know when you are *completely* finished? Use the words *complete* and *completely* in your writing.

_____
_____
_____

Daily Academic Vocabulary

WEEK 33

gather • collect • collection

Use the reproducible definitions on page 189 and the suggestions on page 6 to introduce the words for each day.

DAY 1

gather
(verb) To bring or come together. *We will **gather** at the front of the museum before we go inside.*

Drop five pencils on the floor. Ask: *How can I **gather** these pencils?* (Pick them up and hold them together.) *What might I use to keep them **gathered**?* (e.g., a rubber band; string) *Where might we **gather** as a group that is outside this classroom?* (e.g., playground; library) Conduct the first activity for Day 1 on page 139. Then have students complete the Day 1 activities on their own, in pairs, or as a group.

DAY 2

collect
(verb) To gather together. *I will **collect** your papers at the end of the hour.*

Ask: *What does it mean if I ask you to **collect** your things before you leave?* (Gather your stuff together.) *How can you make sure that you **collect** everything?* (Check the things in your backpack or desk; make a list and check things off.) Conduct the first activity for Day 2 on page 139. Then have students complete the Day 2 activities on their own, in pairs, or as a group.

DAY 3

collection
(noun) A group of things of the same type gathered over time. *He is proud of his **collection** of rare pennies.*

Display a random grouping of items (e.g., stamp; pencil; coin; hat) and a personal **collection**. (e.g., photographs; books; figurines) Have students look at these two groups of items. Ask: *Which of these is a **collection**?* Point to an object in the random grouping that could be collected. Ask: *How could you create a **collection** of ___?* (Gather different ones; find examples of different ones.) Then conduct the first activity for Day 3 on page 140. Have students complete the Day 3 activities on their own, in pairs, or as a group.

DAY 4

collect
(verb) To gather things together as a hobby or to form a collection. *They **collect** stamps that have horses on them.*

Ask: *What are some things that people **collect**?* List them on the board. *If you are interviewing someone who **collects** one of these things, what questions might you ask?* Allow students to suggest questions, such as: "Why do you **collect** snow globes?" "When did you start to **collect** dog food bowls?" Conduct the first activity for Day 4 on page 140. Then have students complete the Day 4 activities on their own, in pairs, or as a group.

DAY 5

Have students complete page 141. Call on students to read aloud their answers to the writing activity.

Name_____

Daily Academic Vocabulary

Day 1 gather

1. How would you complete this sentence? Say it aloud.

   If I went for a walk in the woods, I might gather _____.

2. Three friends *gather* at a playground. Which sentence has the same meaning? Circle your answer.

   a. Three friends describe how to get to a playground.
   b. Three friends walk past a playground.
   c. Three friends leave a playground.
   d. Three friends come together at a playground.

3. If you *gather* berries, what do you do? Circle your answer.

   a. Grow berries.   c. Pick berries.
   b. Eat berries.   d. Plant berries.

Day 2 collect

1. How would you complete this sentence? Say it aloud.

   I am ready to come to school after I collect _____.

2. In which sentence does a teacher *collect* something? Circle your answer.

   a. A teacher gathers together all of the homework papers.
   b. A teacher tells students how to complete the homework.
   c. A teacher asks students to write a poem about nature.
   d. A teacher answers questions about a story.

3. Which of these things can you use to *collect* flowers from a garden? Circle your answers.

a.   b.   c.   d.

© Evan-Moor Corporation • EMC 2758 • Daily Academic Vocabulary

Name_____

Daily Academic Vocabulary

Day 3 collection

1. How would you complete this sentence? Say it aloud.

   I know someone who has a collection of _____.

2. Which sentence describes a *collection*? Circle your answer.

   a. I have more than 15 different rulers.
   b. I use a ruler to measure my desk.
   c. I keep my ruler in my top desk drawer.
   d. I once had a ruler that was made of metal.

3. Which sentence uses *collection* correctly? Circle your answer.

   a. The museum collections rocks and dinosaur bones.
   b. I spent an hour looking at the huge collection of rocks.
   c. I will collection an article about rocks.
   d. I enjoyed the collection of one rock.

Day 4 collect

1. How would you complete this sentence? Say it aloud.

   I would like to collect _____ because _____.

2. Hernando *collects* leaves and puts them in a notebook. What does he do? Circle your answer.

   a. He finds different kinds of leaves and puts them in his notebook.
   b. He takes pages out of his notebook to write poems about leaves.
   c. He uses paper in his notebook to write a story about leaves.
   d. He finds one perfect leaf and glues it into his notebook.

3. What do you do if you *collect* stickers? Circle your answer.

   a. Draw pictures that could be put on stickers.
   b. Forget where you put a sticker.
   c. Gather different stickers as a hobby.
   d. Give away all of your stickers to friends.

Name_____

Day 5 gather • collect • collection

Fill in the bubble next to the correct answer.

1. In which sentence do Jan and her friends *gather* at the library?

Ⓐ Jan tells her friends how to get to the library.
Ⓑ Jan and her friends meet at the library.
Ⓒ Jan brings her friends a book from the library.
Ⓓ Jan and her friends plan to go to the library.

2. If you *collect* seeds, what do you do?

Ⓕ Plant seeds in the ground.
Ⓖ Mail seeds to a friend.
Ⓗ Gather together different seeds.
Ⓙ Throw away seeds from fruits.

3. What is a *collection* of puzzles?

Ⓐ a group of many different puzzles
Ⓑ the answer to a puzzle
Ⓒ a puzzle that you cannot figure out
Ⓓ many pieces from one puzzle

4. Which sentence describes somebody who *collects* something?

Ⓕ Eric reads a book about sled dogs.
Ⓖ Mona has more than 20 maps of Alaska.
Ⓗ Gina learns how to build an igloo.
Ⓙ Hoy visits Alaska with his grandparents.

Writing Imagine that you are at a beach. What things might you *gather* there? What kind of a *collection* might you begin? Use the words *gather* and *collection* in your writing.

_____

_____

_____

Daily Academic Vocabulary

WEEK 34

examine • study

Use the reproducible definitions on page 190 and the suggestions on page 6 to introduce the words for each day.

DAY 1

examine
(verb) To look at something closely and carefully. *The doctor will examine your eyes by looking into them with a bright light.*

Ask students to hold their pencils. Say: **Examine** *the pencil closely. What details do you notice when you* **examine** *a pencil? What tool might help you* **examine** *a pencil?* (magnifying glass) *What is the difference between looking at a pencil and* **examining** *a pencil?* (**Examining** is more thorough and careful.) Conduct the first activity for Day 1 on page 143. Then have students complete the Day 1 activities on their own, in pairs, or as a group.

DAY 2

study
(verb) To examine in detail. *The artist will study the landscape carefully before she begins to paint.*

Say: *Yesterday we learned the word "examine." Examine and* **study** *are synonyms.* Then show students a large photo or poster. Say: *I want you to* **study** *this picture for thirty seconds.* After the time limit, turn the picture around. Ask: *Can you describe what you saw? What details did you find when you* **studied** *the picture?* Display the picture again. Ask: *When you* **study** *the picture again, do you notice any new details?* Conduct the first activity for Day 2 on page 143. Then have students complete the Day 2 activities on their own, in pairs, or as a group.

DAY 3

study
(verb) To learn a subject or skill by reading about it or practicing it. *This year we will study multiplication.*

Ask: *What subjects did you* **study** *last year? What are we* **studying** *this year? What do you think you will* **study** *next year?* Point out that students **study** both general subjects, such as reading and math, as well as specific subjects, such as phonics or fractions. Ask: *What do you like to* **study** *the most? Do you* **study** *anything outside of school?* (e.g., piano; dance; martial arts) Then conduct the first activity for Day 3 on page 144. Have students complete the Day 3 activities on their own, in pairs, or as a group.

DAY 4

study
(noun) A careful examination of something. *Our study of the tree shows that it is very strong and healthy.*

Show students a rock. Ask: *How could you carry out a* **study** *of this rock?* (e.g., look at it closely; rub it against something to see how hard it is; see if it breaks easily) *How would the* **study** *of a bird be different from the* **study** *of a rock?* (You might not be able to touch the bird; you might have to be more patient and watch it from a distance.) Then conduct the first activity for Day 4 on page 144. Have students complete the Day 4 activities on their own, in pairs, or as a group.

DAY 5

Have students complete page 145. Call on students to read aloud their answers to the writing activity.

Name_____

Day 1 examine

1. How would you complete this sentence? Say it aloud.

   I could use a magnifying glass to examine _____.

2. If you *examine* a cactus, what do you do? Circle your answer.

   a. Water it.
   b. Put it in a bigger pot.
   c. Return it to the desert.
   d. Look at it very carefully.

3. In which sentence does Walt *examine* something? Circle your answer.

   a. Walt takes a close look at a silver rock.
   b. Walt collects rocks from a riverbed.
   c. Walt hears the roar of the river.
   d. Walt crosses the river on a wooden bridge.

Day 2 study

1. How would you complete this sentence? Say it aloud.

   If I wanted to study a seashell, I would _____.

2. How can you *study* a ladybug? Circle your answer.

   a. Brush it away.
   b. Look closely at the pattern on its shell.
   c. Bring it to a garden and let it go.
   d. Try not to look at it.

3. In which sentence does somebody *study* something? Circle your answer.

   a. Mary makes a hat out of felt.
   b. Jed borrows a pair of scissors from Helen.
   c. Badra wears a long silk scarf.
   d. Lou examines the pattern on a quilt.

© Evan-Moor Corporation • EMC 2758 • Daily Academic Vocabulary   **WEEK 34**   143

Name _____

Daily Academic Vocabulary

Day 3 study

1. How would you complete this sentence? Say it aloud.

    My favorite subject to study at school is _____.

2. Brian *studies* Spanish. Which sentence has the same meaning? Circle your answer.

    a. Brian speaks only Spanish.
    b. Brian is learning how to speak Spanish.
    c. Brian wants to speak Spanish.
    d. Brian only speaks Spanish at home.

3. What is the best way to *study* penguins? Circle your answer.

    a. Make up stories about penguins.
    b. Make a costume to dress up like a penguin.
    c. Read a book about penguins.
    d. Buy a stuffed penguin at a store.

Day 4 study

1. How would you complete this sentence? Say it aloud.

    Next year in school, I think that we will continue the study of _____.

2. Adam does a *study* of tomatoes. What does he do? Circle your answer.

    a. makes a careful examination of tomatoes
    b. writes a short story about tomato growers
    c. paints a bright red tomato
    d. writes a poem about why he likes tomatoes

3. Which sentence describes the *study* of the planets? Circle your answer.

    a. People wonder if there is life on other planets.
    b. I think that Mars is my favorite planet.
    c. Scientists examine the planets through telescopes.
    d. No one has ever visited Jupiter or Saturn.

I always find the *study* of parrots fascinating!

Name_____

Day 5 examine • study

Fill in the bubble next to the correct answer.

1. How can you *examine* a flower?

  Ⓐ Put it inside a book.
  Ⓑ Look at it carefully.
  Ⓒ Dream about it.
  Ⓓ Imagine it is a different color.

2. If you *study* a rock, what do you do?

  Ⓕ Throw it into the ocean.
  Ⓖ Give it to someone.
  Ⓗ Tie a long string around it.
  Ⓙ Notice the details of what it looks like.

3. In which sentence does Tasha *study* something?

  Ⓐ Tasha tells her sister a story about clouds.
  Ⓑ Tasha carries a flashlight in her backpack.
  Ⓒ Tasha learns about electricity at school.
  Ⓓ Tasha draws a picture of Benjamin Franklin.

4. What might the *study* of butterflies include?

  Ⓕ Watching butterflies very closely.
  Ⓖ Making up stories about butterflies.
  Ⓗ Thinking of other topics you would rather explore.
  Ⓙ Pretending that you are a butterfly.

Writing What subject in science would you like to *study?* What is something you might *examine* if you *study* this subject? Use the words *study* and *examine* in your writing.

_____

_____

_____

Daily Academic Vocabulary

WEEK 35

rule • require • requirement

Use the reproducible definitions on page 191 and the suggestions on page 6 to introduce the words for each day.

DAY 1

rule
(verb) To have power over something or someone. *Kings should **rule** their countries fairly.*

Have students imagine a day on which students **rule** the school. Ask: *What would this day be like? How would you **rule** the school? What would you do? Who **rules** the school on other days? Do you think **ruling** school would be fun or hard work?* Conduct the first activity for Day 1 on page 147. Then have students complete the Day 1 activities on their own, in pairs, or as a group.

DAY 2

rule
(noun) An instruction that tells you how you must act or how something is done. *There is a **rule** that dogs are not allowed in the store.*

Say: *Sometimes a **rule** tells people how they are to behave. What **rules** do we have at school? What other places have **rules**?* (libraries; swimming pools) *What is one **rule** you have at home? What is one traffic **rule**?* Then say: *A **rule** can also tell how something works or is done. For example, in math there is a **rule** that says numbers can be added in any order.* Ask: *Who can state a **rule** we use when we write a sentence?* (begin with a capital letter; end with a punctuation mark) Conduct the first activity for Day 2 on page 147. Then have students complete the Day 2 activities on their own, in pairs, or as a group.

DAY 3

rule
(noun) Something that usually or normally happens. *As a **rule**, we have a spelling test on Thursday.*

Ask: *What are some things that are the **rule**, or usually happen, in our classroom first thing in the morning? I could say, "It's the **rule** to turn in homework at the beginning of the school day."* Then ask: *What are some other things we do at school as a **rule**?* Invite students to share ideas, beginning their sentences with, "As a **rule**..." Conduct the first activity for Day 3 on page 148. Have students complete the Day 3 activities on their own, in pairs, or as a group.

DAY 4

require
(verb) To have need of something. *We **require** a telescope to see the comet.*

requirement
(noun) Something that you need to do or have to do. *Taking off your shoes is a **requirement** in some homes.*

Draw a picture of a tent on the board. Say: *Imagine that you are going camping. What would you **require** for your trip?* (e.g., a tent, food, sleeping bags) *Would matches be a **requirement** for your trip?* (Yes.) *Would a basketball be a **requirement**?* (No.) *When is a basketball a **requirement**?* (when you want to play basketball) *What else do you **require** to play basketball?* (a hoop; space) Then ask: *What is a **requirement** at your home?* Conduct the first activity for Day 4 on page 148. Then have students complete the Day 4 activities on their own, in pairs, or as a group.

DAY 5

Have students complete page 149. Call on students to read aloud their answers to the writing activity.

Name _____

Day 1 rule

1. **How would you complete this sentence? Say it aloud.**

    If I could rule my neighborhood for a day, I would _____.

2. **What does it mean if a queen *rules* a country? Circle your answer.**

    a. She leaves the country.
    b. She was born in the country but now lives somewhere else.
    c. She describes what her country is like.
    d. She has power over people in the country.

3. **Which sentence describes someone who *rules* someone else? Circle your answer.**

    a. The baby plays a silly game with a neighbor.
    b. The baby sitter makes decisions for the two-year-old child.
    c. The mayor walks through town with the police captain.
    d. The president listens to the mayor making a speech.

Day 2 rule

1. **How would you complete these sentences? Say them aloud.**

    I agree with the rule that says _____.

    One punctuation rule I know is _____.

2. **Steven explains the *rules* at the zoo. What does he do? Circle your answer.**

    a. He feeds the animals after the visitors go home.
    b. He tells people the difference between alligators and crocodiles.
    c. He explains where people can find different kinds of animals.
    d. He tells people what they can and cannot do at the zoo.

3. **Which of the following is a subtraction *rule*? Circle your answer.**

    a. Any number minus zero is the number itself.
    b. I think subtraction is harder than addition.
    c. We will learn more about subtraction later this year.
    d. People use subtraction every day when they go shopping.

Name _____

Daily Academic Vocabulary

Day 3 rule

1. **How would you complete this sentence? Say it aloud.**

    At my house, it's the rule to _____ on Saturday.

2. **Which of these might be the *rule* for a student to do in the library? Circle your answer.**

    a. fall asleep at the table   c. sing loudly
    b. check out a book   d. take all the books off the shelves

3. **As a *rule*, our teacher doesn't give homework on Friday. Which sentence has the same meaning? Circle your answer.**

    a. The teacher tells us to do homework on Friday.
    b. We finish our homework on Sunday.
    c. We do not have homework on Saturday and Sunday.
    d. We never have any homework.

Day 4 require • requirement

1. **How would you complete these sentences? Say them aloud.**

    If I were going to paint a picture, I would require _____.

    One requirement for playing soccer is _____.

2. **Mieko *requires* a cup of flour for a recipe. Which sentence has the same meaning? Circle your answer.**

    a. Mieko needs a cup of flour for a recipe.
    b. Mieko finds a cup of flour for a recipe.
    c. Mieko measures a cup of flour for a recipe.
    d. Mieko leaves out a cup of flour for a recipe.

3. **Which of these things are a *requirement* for playing baseball? Circle your answers.**

  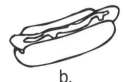

a.   b.   c.   d.

148 WEEK 35   Daily Academic Vocabulary • EMC 2758 • © Evan-Moor Corporation

Name_____

Day 5 rule • require • requirement

Fill in the bubble next to the correct answer.

1. A judge *rules* a courtroom. What does this mean?

   Ⓐ The judge has power over people in the courtroom.
   Ⓑ The judge cannot talk to people in the courtroom.
   Ⓒ The judge makes decisions based on facts.
   Ⓓ The judge paints the courtroom in order to make it brighter.

2. What does a *rule* tell you?

   Ⓕ how to make important decisions
   Ⓖ why something happened
   Ⓗ how you can find the answers to difficult problems
   Ⓙ how you must act or how something is done

3. When going on a hike, wearing _____ is the *rule*.

   Ⓐ a swimsuit and a towel
   Ⓑ kneepads and a helmet
   Ⓒ jeans and sturdy shoes
   Ⓓ pajamas and slippers

4. What is one *requirement* for riding a bicycle?

   Ⓕ a helmet
   Ⓖ a bright green shirt
   Ⓗ a car
   Ⓙ a rainy day

Writing Pretend you are going to the moon. What is one *rule* you would probably have to follow? What is one thing you would *require* for your trip? Use the words *rule* and *require* in your writing.

_____

_____

_____

CUMULATIVE REVIEW
WORDS FROM WEEKS 28–35

collect
collection
complete
completely
completion
examine
gather
locate
located
location
observation
observe
plan
position
prepare
require
requirement
restate
rule
state
statement
study

Days 1–4
Each day's activity is a cloze paragraph that students complete with words or forms of words that they have learned in weeks 28–35. Before students begin, pronounce each word in the box on the student page, have students repeat each word, and then review each word's meaning(s). **Other ways to review the words:**

- Start a sentence containing one of the words and have students finish the sentence orally. For example:

    *I would like to have a **collection** of…*
    *The Amazon Rainforest is **located** in…*

- Provide students with a definition and ask them to supply the word that fits it.

- Ask questions that require students to know the meaning of each word. For example:

    *Where might you **observe** a penguin?*
    *What is one **requirement** for being a doctor?*
    *How can you **prepare** to play soccer?*

- Have students use each word in a sentence.

Day 5
Start by reviewing the words not practiced on Days 1–4: **collect**, **completion**, **examine**, **observation**, **statement**. Write the words on the board and have students repeat them after you. Provide a sentence for one of the words. Ask students to think of their own sentence and share it with a partner. Call on several students to share their sentences. Follow the same procedure for the remaining words. Then have students complete the code-breaker activity.

Extension Ideas
Use any of the following activities to help integrate the vocabulary words into other content areas:

- Ask students to conduct an **observation** of a common flower, such as a daisy. After they **examine** it, ask them to write a **statement** about it.

- Have students **study** a map of South America to find the name and **location** of each country. Suggest that small groups **prepare** a game to help learn the countries and demonstrate it for the class.

- Have students **gather** ten objects found in nature and use those objects to create a new insect. Ask them what the insect does and what it **requires** for food and shelter.

- Have students **collect** examples of numbers in newspapers and magazines. Ask them to **state** where each number was **located** and how it was used.

Name _____

Daily Academic Vocabulary

| gather | located | observe | positions | state |
| locate | location | plan | requirement | |

Day 1

Fill in the blanks with words from the word box.

The Atlantic Ocean is _____ along the eastern coasts of North and South America. Do you know the _____ of the Pacific Ocean? All oceans contain salt water. Some scientists _____ ocean water very carefully. They _____ information about chemicals in the water. They want to find out if the _____ of the ocean is healthy.

Day 2

Fill in the blanks with words from the word box.

Practice is a _____ if you want to play a musical instrument. No one plays perfectly right away. For example, to play a flute, you need to learn the correct _____ for your fingers. To play a guitar, you need to _____ the correct strings. To learn any instrument, you should _____ to spend some time practicing every day.

WEEK 36

Name_____

Daily Academic Vocabulary

| collection | completely | require | rules |
| complete | prepare | restate | study |

Day 3

Fill in the blanks with words from the word box.

Poetry can be fun to read. Sometimes, you might not _____ understand the poem the first time you read it. That's no problem! Just read it again. Try to _____ the ideas in your own words. If you really like a poem, copy it down. You can keep your _____ of favorite poems in a folder. You can use crayons or markers to _____ a cover as beautiful as the poems inside.

Day 4

Fill in the blanks with words from the word box.

What _____ do you follow at the library? You might speak quietly so that other people can _____. You should also handle books with care. Most libraries _____ you to have a library card to borrow books. You can check out books you want to read at home. You might even read the _____ set of books in a series. Best of all, most libraries are free!

Name _____

Day 5

Crack the Code!

Write one of the words from the word box on the lines next to each clue.

collect	completion	located	plan	requirement	state
collection	examine	location	position	restate	statement
complete	gather	observation	prepare	rule	study
completely	locate	observe	require		

1. to get ready

   ___ ___ ___ ___ ___ ___ ___
      1

2. the end of something

   ___ ___ ___ ___ ___ ___ ___ ___ ___ ___
      2

3. something that is put into words

   ___ ___ ___ ___ ___ ___ ___ ___ ___
                  3

4. to look at closely

   ___ ___ ___ ___ ___ ___ ___
               4

5. to gather together

   ___ ___ ___ ___ ___ ___ ___
              5

6. something that is seen

   ___ ___ ___ ___ ___ ___ ___ ___ ___ ___ ___
      6

Now use the numbers under the letters to crack the code.
Write the letters on the lines below. The words will solve this riddle.

Where is the ocean the deepest?

___ ___ ___ h ___ ___ ___ ___ ___ ___
 2 4   5   1   6 2 5 5 2 3

© Evan-Moor Corporation • EMC 2758 • Daily Academic Vocabulary   **WEEK 36**   153

Index

agree 38, 42
agreement 38, 42
alike 22, 42
amount 70, 78
appear 54, 78
appearance 54, 78
belief 102, 114
believe 102, 114
choice 50, 78
choose 50, 78
clue 102, 114
collect 138, 150
collection 138, 150
combination 26, 42
combine 26, 42
common 18, 42
compare 82, 114
comparison 82, 114
complete 134, 150
completely 134, 150
completion 134, 150
connect 26, 42
connection 26, 42
copy 110, 114
correct 30, 42
correction 30, 42
create 62, 78
creation 62, 78
different 82, 114
direct 106, 114
direction 106, 114
directions 106, 114
disagree 38, 42
equal 22, 42
examine 142, 150

example 34, 42
explain 34, 42
fact 10, 42
figure 66, 78
figure out 66, 78
gather 138, 150
group 46, 78
hint 102, 114
image 58, 78
imaginary 58, 78
imagination 58, 78
imagine 58, 78
importance 14, 42
important 14, 42
improve 74, 78
improvement 74, 78
in common 18, 42
indirect 106, 114
invent 62, 78
invention 62, 78
item 46, 78
know 98, 114
knowledge 98, 114
list 46, 78
locate 130, 150
located 130, 150
location 130, 150
main 14, 42
measure 70, 78
measurement 70, 78
measures 70, 78
minor 14, 42
observation 126, 150
observe 126, 150
opinion 10, 42

pattern 110, 114
place 86, 114
plan 122, 150
position 130, 150
prepare 122, 150
record 90, 114
remove 86, 114
replace 86, 114
reply 94, 114
report 94, 114
require 146, 150
requirement 146, 150
restate 118, 150
result 90, 114
rule 146, 150
similar 82, 114
solution 66, 78
solve 66, 78
special 18, 42
state 118, 150
statement 118, 150
study 142, 150
success 74, 78
successful 74, 78
test 10, 42
trace 110, 114
uncommon 18, 42
unlike 22, 42

Daily Academic Vocabulary — Week 1

fact — DAY 1

(noun) Something that is known to be true or to have really happened.

*It's a **fact** that there are twelve months in a year.*

opinion — DAY 2

(noun) A belief or idea about something.

*In my **opinion**, ice cream is the best dessert.*

test — DAY 3

(verb) To try something out in order to judge it or to find out more about it.

*I sat on the bike and **tested** the height to see if it was the right size for me.*

test — DAY 4

(noun) A set of questions to find out how much someone knows about something.

*We had a surprise **test** on our number facts this morning.*

Daily Academic Vocabulary — Week 2

important
DAY 1

(adj.) Having great value, meaning, or influence.

*Learning to spell is **important**.*

importance
DAY 2

(noun) The condition of being important.

*The dentist told us about the **importance** of brushing our teeth.*

main
DAY 3

(adj.) Most important.

*The **main** idea of the book is that friendships are valuable.*

minor
DAY 4

(adj.) Small in importance or size.

*The actor had a **minor** part in the play and only appeared once.*

Daily Academic Vocabulary — Week 3

common — DAY 1

(adj.) Happening often. *The school bus is a **common** way to get to school.*

common • in common — DAY 2

common
(adj.) Shared by two or more things or people; shared by each and all. *My brother and I have a **common** interest in swimming.*

in common
(phrase) Shared by two or more things or people; shared by each and all. *My new neighbor and I have many things **in common**.*

uncommon — DAY 3

(adj.) Not happening often. *It is **uncommon** to see a purple car.*

special — DAY 4

(adj.) Different from other things or people. *I gave my mother the **special** scarf I made.*

Daily Academic Vocabulary — Week 4

equal — DAY 1

(adj.) The same in size, value, or amount.

*Four quarters and one dollar are **equal** amounts.*

equal — DAY 2

(verb) To be the same as, or equal to, something else.

*Two dimes and a nickel **equal** a quarter.*

alike — DAY 3

(adj.) Looking or acting the same way.

*These pictures are **alike** because they are both drawings of a daisy.*

unlike — DAY 4

(prep.) Different.

*This rock is **unlike** the others because it is shiny.*

Daily Academic Vocabulary — Week 5

combine — DAY 1

(verb) To bring together or join together into a whole.

*When you **combine** lemons, sugar, and water, you make lemonade.*

combination — DAY 2

(noun) Things that have come together or have been brought together.

*The **combination** of peanut butter and jelly makes a delicious sandwich!*

connect — DAY 3

(verb) To join together or link.

*The sidewalks **connect** the two buildings of our school.*

connection — DAY 4

(noun) A link or relationship between two things.

*There is a **connection** between eating healthy food and feeling good.*

Daily Academic Vocabulary — Week 6

correct — DAY 1

(verb) To fix mistakes in something or make it right.

*Proofread your paper and **correct** any spelling mistakes.*

correct — DAY 2

(adj.) Having no mistakes.

*That answer is **correct**.*

correct — DAY 3

(verb) To mark errors or point out mistakes in something.

*Our teacher will **correct** our spelling papers and give us a grade.*

correction — DAY 4

(noun) Something put in the place of something wrong.

*I misspelled the word, so I erased it and made a **correction**.*

Daily Academic Vocabulary — Week 7

explain — DAY 1

(verb) To tell about something in a way that is easy to understand.

*The teacher will **explain** how to do the science experiment.*

explain — DAY 2

(verb) To give a reason why.

*The boy should **explain** why he was late to school.*

example — DAY 3

(noun) Something that is picked out to show what other things of its type or group are like.

*A lemon is an **example** of something that is sour.*

example — DAY 4

(noun) A problem that is worked out in order to show how to answer other problems of this type.

*The **example** helped me figure out how to solve the math problem.*

Daily Academic Vocabulary — Week 8

agree — DAY 1

(verb) To think the same way about something.

*My sister and I **agree** that summer is the best season.*

agree — DAY 2

(verb) To say yes to something.

*We **agree** to help our father clean the house.*

agreement — DAY 3

(noun) An understanding between two or more persons or groups.

*The club members made an **agreement** to meet once a week.*

disagree — DAY 4

(verb) To have a different feeling or belief from someone else.

*My friend and I **disagree** about who is the best singer in our class.*

Daily Academic Vocabulary — Week 10

list — DAY 1

(verb) To say or write down things that fit in a group. — *The teacher will **list** the names of students in our class.*

(noun) A set of things that are written down. — *Mom made a **list** of clothes to buy for school.*

item — DAY 2

(noun) One of a number of things. — *We made a list of each **item** we needed at the store.*

group — DAY 3

(noun) A number of persons or things that go together or are put together. — *Ms. Wong showed the **group** of new students around the school.*

group — DAY 4

(verb) To put persons or things together in a group. — *The principal will **group** the students by grade.*

Daily Academic Vocabulary — Week 11

choose — DAY 1

(verb) To pick from a group.

*I **choose** Tess to be my reading buddy today.*

choice — DAY 2

(noun) The thing or person that is selected.

*That song was Kelsey's **choice** for the talent show.*

choice — DAY 3

(noun) The right or chance to choose.

*It was my **choice** to go to the park instead of the movies.*

choice — DAY 4

(noun) A number of things to choose or pick from.

*The menu gives us a **choice** of vegetables.*

Daily Academic Vocabulary — Week 12

appear — DAY 1

(verb) To seem to be.

*Sometimes things **appear** to be different than they really are.*

appear — DAY 2

(verb) To come into view.

*The sun will **appear** from behind the clouds.*

appearance — DAY 3

(noun) The act of coming into view.

*A clown made an **appearance** at the party.*

appearance — DAY 4

(noun) The way that something or somebody looks.

*The **appearance** of the school was clean and neat.*

Daily Academic Vocabulary — Week 13

image — DAY 1

(noun) A picture of a person or thing.
*The painting shows an **image** of a horse racing across a desert.*

(noun) A picture of something in the mind.
*When I think of summer, the **image** of the beach comes to my mind.*

imagine — DAY 2

(verb) To picture something in your mind.
*Sometimes I like to **imagine** that I am an astronaut on Mars.*

imagination — DAY 3

(noun) The talent to picture things in the mind.
*Ramon's stories show what a good **imagination** he has.*

imaginary — DAY 4

(adj.) Not real.
*An elf is an **imaginary** creature.*

Daily Academic Vocabulary — Week 14

invent
DAY 1

(verb) To make up or think of something new.

*Someone might **invent** a flying car.*

invention
DAY 2

(noun) Something that is invented.

*The computer is a useful **invention**.*

create
DAY 3

(verb) To make or design something.

*An artist can **create** a painting.*

(verb) To cause to happen.

*The baby will **create** a mess with her food.*

creation
DAY 4

(noun) Something that has been made.

*Ana's favorite **creation** is a model volcano she made last year.*

Daily Academic Vocabulary

Week 15

solve
DAY 1

(verb) To find an answer to a problem.

*Tamara will **solve** the math problem by adding two numbers together.*

solution
DAY 2

(noun) The answer to a problem.

*I found the **solution** to the word problem by using subtraction.*

figure • figure out
DAY 3

figure

(verb) To work something out by using numbers.

*I will **figure** the cost of our lunch on my calculator.*

figure out

(verb) To solve something by thinking about it.

*I know you can **figure out** the riddle if you keep working on it.*

figure
DAY 4

(noun) An outline, form, or shape.

*I see the **figure** of a crouching lion in the cloud.*

Daily Academic Vocabulary — Week 16

amount — DAY 1

(noun) How much there is of something.

*The **amount** of flour you need to make the cake is 4 cups.*

measure — DAY 2

(verb) To find the length, size, weight, or amount of something.

*Will you **measure** my height?*

measures — DAY 3

(verb) To provide a way of measuring.

*A thermometer **measures** temperature.*

measurement — DAY 4

(noun) The length, size, weight, or amount of something.

*Please take an exact **measurement** of the window.*

Daily Academic Vocabulary — Week 17

improve
DAY 1

(verb) To get better, or to make something better.

*He will **improve** his story if he adds a surprise ending.*

improvement
DAY 2

(noun) A change that makes something better.

*Painting the wall yellow will be a great **improvement**.*

success
DAY 3

(noun) A person who does well, or something that goes well.

*Rob's science experiment was a **success**.*

successful
DAY 4

(adj.) Ending or going well; having success.

*The students were **successful** in learning their spelling words.*

Daily Academic Vocabulary — Week 19

different — DAY 1

(adj.) Not the same; unlike something else.

*My sister's straight hair is very **different** from my curly hair.*

similar — DAY 2

(adj.) Alike but not exactly the same as something else.

*A baseball is **similar** to a softball, except it is smaller.*

compare — DAY 3

(verb) To judge how two or more things are different and alike.

*I will **compare** the two shirts before I decide which one to buy.*

comparison — DAY 4

(noun) The act of judging how two or more things are different and alike.

*A quick **comparison** shows me that this book is longer than that one.*

Daily Academic Vocabulary — Week 20

place — DAY 1

(noun) A specific area or location.

*This is the perfect **place** for a picnic.*

place — DAY 2

(noun) Position or order.

*I won a ribbon for coming in second **place**.*

place • replace — DAY 3

place
(verb) To put in a specific spot or location.

***Place** the picnic basket on the table.*

replace
(verb) To put one thing or person in the place of another.

*Dylan is ill, so Sarah will **replace** him as line leader.*

remove — DAY 4

(verb) To take something off or away.

*When we enter the classroom, we **remove** our jackets and hang them up.*

Daily Academic Vocabulary — Week 21

record — DAY 1

(noun) Information or facts that are written down.

*We kept a **record** of each day's weather.*

record — DAY 2

(verb) To write something down so that it can be kept.

*We **record** the weather on our weather chart each day.*

result — DAY 3

(noun) Something that happens because something else happens.

*That muddy puddle is one **result** of yesterday's rain.*

result — DAY 4

(verb) To happen from a cause.

*A stain can **result** from spilled juice.*

Daily Academic Vocabulary

Week 22

reply
DAY 1

(verb) To give or say an answer or response.

*The teacher will **reply** to questions from the students.*

reply
DAY 2

(noun) An answer or response.

*Her **reply** to the question was clear and correct.*

report
DAY 3

(noun) A written or spoken description of something.

*He is writing a **report** on different kinds of volcanoes.*

report
DAY 4

(verb) To give a written or spoken description of something.

*The student **reports** to his parents what he did in school.*

Daily Academic Vocabulary — Week 23

know — DAY 1

(verb) To be certain about the facts or that something is true.

*I **know** that a triangle has three corners and three sides.*

know — DAY 2

(verb) To be familiar with a person, place, or thing.

*My best friend and I **know** each other very well.*

know — DAY 3

(verb) To have skill in doing something.

*Eduardo **knows** how to speak English and Spanish.*

knowledge — DAY 4

(noun) The things that one understands from having done them or studied them.

*Her **knowledge** of soccer comes from playing the sport for many years.*

Daily Academic Vocabulary — Week 24

believe — DAY 1

(verb) To feel that something is true, real, or important.

*I **believe** dogs are the best pets.*

belief — DAY 2

(noun) Something that one feels is true or real.

*It is his **belief** that soccer is the best sport.*

clue — DAY 3

(noun) A piece of information that helps one solve a problem or mystery.

*Karen used the **clues** to solve the riddle.*

hint — DAY 4

(noun) A slight suggestion or helpful tip.

*Please give me a **hint** to help me solve this math problem.*

(verb) To give a slight suggestion about something.

*I will **hint** that I would like a game for my birthday.*

Daily Academic Vocabulary   Week 25

direct   DAY 1

(verb) To tell which way to go or what to do.   *The museum guard can **direct** you to the dinosaur room.*

direct • indirect   DAY 2

direct
(adj.) Going in a straight line.   *He pitches the ball in a **direct** path to the batter.*

---

indirect
(adj.) Not in a straight line.   *The bus route from my house to school is **indirect** because it winds all over town.*

direction   DAY 3

(noun) The way that someone or something is moving or pointing.   *The road sign showed the **direction** to New Town.*

directions   DAY 4

(noun) Instructions on how to do something.   *The **directions** told us how to put the tent together.*

© Evan-Moor Corporation • EMC 2758 • Daily Academic Vocabulary

Daily Academic Vocabulary — Week 26

pattern — DAY 1

(noun) A repeating arrangement of colors, shapes, numbers, sounds, or other things.

*The rhyming **pattern** of the poem made it easy to learn.*

pattern — DAY 2

(noun) Actions or events that always happen in the same way or in the same order.

*Our family's activities on Sunday always follow the same **pattern**.*

copy — DAY 3

(noun) Something that looks or sounds exactly like another thing.

*I have a **copy** of the famous painting Sunflowers.*

(verb) To write the exact words.

*Please **copy** this sentence from the board.*

trace — DAY 4

(verb) To copy a picture or shape by following its outline.

*We **trace** each letter before we write it.*

Daily Academic Vocabulary

Week 28

state — DAY 1

(noun) The condition of a person or thing.

*He was in a **state** of shock when his Earth Day poster won first place.*

state — DAY 2

(verb) To use words to say, tell, or explain.

*Please **state** your name clearly so we can hear you.*

statement — DAY 3

(noun) Something that is put into words.

*I agree with everything she said in her **statement**.*

restate — DAY 4

(verb) To say again in a new way or to repeat.

*The judge will **restate** the law in simpler words to help us understand it.*

Daily Academic Vocabulary — Week 29

plan — DAY 1

(noun) An idea worked out ahead of time about how to do something.

*Our **plan** is to go on a hike tomorrow.*

(verb) To work out ahead of time how to do something.

*We **plan** how we will decorate for the party.*

plan — DAY 2

(verb) To mean to do something.

*I **plan** to read the last chapter of my book tonight.*

prepare — DAY 3

(verb) To make or get yourself ready.

*We **prepare** for the party by making our costumes.*

prepare — DAY 4

(verb) To put parts or ingredients together to make something.

*Mara can **prepare** breakfast for herself and her brother.*

Daily Academic Vocabulary — Week 30

observe
DAY 1

(verb) To watch someone or something closely.

*The owls **observe** the mice on the ground.*

observation
DAY 2

(noun) The careful watching of something.

*Our **observation** of the seed sprouting helped us understand how plants grow.*

observe
DAY 3

(verb) To notice something by looking or watching.

*As I look around the playground, I **observe** two girls jumping rope.*

observation
DAY 4

(noun) Something that is noticed or seen.

*Please share your **observations** of the ants.*

Daily Academic Vocabulary — Week 31

position — DAY 1

(noun) The place where someone or something is.

*Please move those books to a new **position** so they are not in the way.*

locate — DAY 2

(verb) To find out where something or someone is.

*Will you help the new student **locate** the library?*

located — DAY 3

(verb) To be placed or found in a certain spot.

*Rome is **located** in Italy.*

location — DAY 4

(noun) The place or position where something is.

*The school office is in a nearby **location**.*

Daily Academic Vocabulary — Week 32

complete • completely — DAY 1

complete
(adj.) Having all the needed parts; whole.
*I found the missing piece, so the puzzle is **complete** again.*

completely
(adv.) Totally.
*She filled in the form **completely**, making sure there were no blank spaces left.*

complete — DAY 2

(verb) To finish or end.
*Tonight I will **complete** the book I have been reading.*

complete — DAY 3

(verb) To add what is missing.
*We can **complete** the sentence by adding the missing verb.*

completion — DAY 4

(noun) The act of bringing something to a finish or end.
*An awards assembly will celebrate the **completion** of our school year.*

© Evan-Moor Corporation • EMC 2758 • Daily Academic Vocabulary

Daily Academic Vocabulary — Week 33

gather
DAY 1

(verb) To bring or come together.

*We will **gather** at the front of the museum before we go inside.*

collect
DAY 2

(verb) To gather together.

*I will **collect** your papers at the end of the hour.*

collection
DAY 3

(noun) A group of things of the same type gathered over time.

*He is proud of his **collection** of rare pennies.*

collect
DAY 4

(verb) To gather things together as a hobby or to form a collection.

*They **collect** stamps that have horses on them.*

Daily Academic Vocabulary — Week 34

examine — DAY 1

(verb) To look at something closely and carefully.

*The doctor will **examine** your eyes by looking into them with a bright light.*

study — DAY 2

(verb) To examine in detail.

*The artist will **study** the landscape carefully before she begins to paint.*

study — DAY 3

(verb) To learn a subject or skill by reading about it or practicing it.

*This year we will **study** multiplication.*

study — DAY 4

(noun) A careful examination of something.

*Our **study** of the tree shows that it is very strong and healthy.*

Daily Academic Vocabulary — Week 35

rule — DAY 1

(verb) To have power over something or someone.

*Kings should **rule** their countries fairly.*

rule — DAY 2

(noun) An instruction that tells you how you must act or how something is done.

*There is a **rule** that dogs are not allowed in the store.*

rule — DAY 3

(noun) Something that usually or normally happens.

*As a **rule**, we have a spelling test on Thursday.*

require • requirement — DAY 4

require

(verb) To have need of something.

*We **require** a telescope to see the comet.*

requirement

(noun) Something that you need to do or have to do.

*Taking off your shoes is a **requirement** in some homes.*

Answer Key

Week 1
Day 1
2. a, c
3. b

Day 2
2. d
3. a, b

Day 3
2. c
3. a

Day 4
2. d
3. a

Day 5
1. A 2. H 3. B 4. J

Week 2
Day 1
2. a, d
3. a, c

Day 2
2. c
3. b

Day 3
2. Answers will vary.
3. a, c

Day 4
2. b
3. d

Day 5
1. B 2. J 3. D 4. H

Week 3
Day 1
2. a, c
3. b

Day 2
2. a, c
3. d

Day 3
2. b
3. c

Day 4
2. c
3. b

Day 5
1. A 2. H 3. B 4. G

Week 4
Day 1
2. c
3. d

Day 2
2. b
3. b, c

Day 3
2. a, d
3. c

Day 4
2. c
3. c

Day 5
1. A 2. G 3. C 4. J

Week 5
Day 1
2. d
3. b

Day 2
2. b
3. c

Day 3
2. a
3. b

Day 4
2. b, d
3. b

Day 5
1. A 2. J 3. A 4. H

Week 6
Day 1
2. d
3. c

Day 2
2. a
3. d

Day 3
2. d
3. c

Day 4
2. b
3. a, d

Day 5
1. B 2. J 3. B 4. F

Week 7
Day 1
2. c
3. Answers will vary.

Day 2
2. a
3. Answers will vary.

Day 3
2. c
3. a

Day 4
2. a
3. Answers will vary.

Day 5
1. B 2. H 3. B 4. G

Week 8
Day 1
2. c
3. d

Day 2
2. d
3. Answers will vary.

Day 3
2. d
3. b

Day 4
2. c
3. a

Day 5
1. D 2. F 3. C 4. H

Week 9 Review
Day 1
connection, in common, example, important
Day 2
agreement, facts, combine, correct
Day 3
explain, main, opinion, uncommon
Day 4
combination, minor, corrections, agree
Day 5
Down
  1. unlike
  3. equals
  5. special
  6. test
Across
  2. connect
  4. common
  7. importance
  8. alike
  9. disagree

Week 10
Day 1
 2. d
 3. c
Day 2
 2. a, c
 3. Answers will vary.
Day 3
 2. b
 3. a
Day 4
 2. c, d
 3. a
Day 5
 1. C 2. F 3. D 4. F

Week 11
Day 1
 2. b
 3. Answers will vary.
Day 2
 2. a, c
 3. c
Day 3
 2. Answers will vary.
 3. c
Day 4
 2. c
 3. a
Day 5
 1. B 2. H 3. D 4. F

Week 12
Day 1
 2. c
 3. d
Day 2
 2. a, d
 3. a
Day 3
 2. a
 3. d
Day 4
 2. b, c
 3. a
Day 5
 1. A 2. H 3. C 4. G

Week 13
Day 1
 2. a
 3. d
Day 2
 2. d
 3. c
Day 3
 2. b
 3. d
Day 4
 2. c
 3. a
Day 5
 1. B 2. J 3. C 4. F

Week 14
Day 1
 2. b
 3. c
Day 2
 2. c, d
 3. c
Day 3
 2. a
 3. c
Day 4
 2. d
 3. a
Day 5
 1. D 2. G 3. B 4. J

Week 15
Day 1
 2. b, c
 3. a
Day 2
 2. d
 3. b
Day 3
 2. b
 3. c
Day 4
 2. a, c
 3. b, d
Day 5
 1. D 2. H 3. A 4. F

Week 16
Day 1
 2. b, d
 3. b
Day 2
 2. c, d
 3. a, c
Day 3
 2. b, c
 3. a
Day 4
 2. a, c
 3. c

Day 5
1. B   2. J   3. A   4. J

Week 17
Day 1
2. a, c
3. b, d

Day 2
2. b
3. a

Day 3
2. a
3. a, d

Day 4
2. c
3. d

Day 5
1. A   2. H   3. D   4. H

Week 18 Review
Day 1
appearance, group, imagine, choose

Day 2
invention, figure out, improve, success, imagination, successful

Day 3
solve, measure, list, item, measurement

Day 4
create, choice, figure, appears, imaginary, improvement

Day 5
1. creation
2. amount
3. invent
4. image
5. solution
6. improve
Code: tomato paste

Week 19
Day 1
2. b, c
3. c, d

Day 2
2. a, d
3. b

Day 3
2. a, d
3. c

Day 4
2. a
3. b

Day 5
1. A   2. J   3. D   4. G

Week 20
Day 1
2. a, c
3. a

Day 2
2. c
3. d

Day 3
2. a
3. c

Day 4
2. c
3. a

Day 5
1. D   2. J   3. C   4. G

Week 21
Day 1
2. a, d
3. c

Day 2
2. b, d
3. b, c

Day 3
2. c
3. a

Day 4
2. d
3. b

Day 5
1. B   2. F   3. C   4. H

Week 22
Day 1
2. c, d
3. a, c

Day 2
2. b, d
3. d

Day 3
2. c
3. c, d

Day 4
2. c
3. b

Day 5
1. D   2. H   3. A   4. F

Week 23
Day 1
2. b
3. a, d

Day 2
2. d
3. c

Day 3
2. c
3. a

Day 4
2. d
3. c

Day 5
1. C   2. F   3. D   4. F

Week 24
Day 1
2. c
3. b

Day 2
2. a
3. c

Day 3
  2. b, c
  3. c
Day 4
  2. b
  3. a, c
Day 5
  1. C   2. H   3. D   4. G

Week 25
Day 1
  2. c, d
  3. d
Day 2
  2. c
  3. a, c
Day 3
  2. c
  3. a
Day 4
  2. c
  3. a, d
Day 5
  1. B   2. H   3. A   4. G

Week 26
Day 1
  2. d
  3. d
Day 2
  2. b
  3. a
Day 3
  2. b
  3. c
Day 4
  2. a
  3. d
Day 5
  1. B   2. H   3. A   4. H

Week 27 Review
Day 1
  remove, place, directions, result, know

Day 2
  pattern, compare, different, record
Day 3
  believe, similar, reply, trace
Day 4
  direction, knowledge, direct, indirect
Day 5
  Across
    1. different
    3. copy
    4. replace
    6. clues
    7. hint
    8. knowledge
  Down
    2. report
    3. comparison
    5. belief

Week 28
Day 1
  2. a, d
  3. d
Day 2
  2. d
  3. d
Day 3
  2. a
  3. c
Day 4
  2. a
  3. b
Day 5
  1. B   2. G   3. C   4. H

Week 29
Day 1
  2. d
  3. a
Day 2
  2. a
  3. c

Day 3
  2. b
  3. c
Day 4
  2. a, d
  3. b
Day 5
  1. B   2. H   3. B   4. F

Week 30
Day 1
  2. c
  3. a
Day 2
  2. a
  3. c
Day 3
  2. a
  3. c
Day 4
  2. b
  3. d
Day 5
  1. C   2. J   3. B   4. G

Week 31
Day 1
  2. a
  3. c
Day 2
  2. d
  3. c
Day 3
  2. c
  3. b
Day 4
  2. d
  3. a
Day 5
  1. A   2. H   3. C   4. G

Week 32
Day 1
  2. c
  3. a

Day 2
 2. d
 3. b
Day 3
 2. b
 3. b
Day 4
 2. d
 3. a
Day 5
 1. C   2. F   3. D   4. F

Week 33

Day 1
 2. d
 3. c
Day 2
 2. a
 3. a, d
Day 3
 2. a
 3. b
Day 4
 2. a
 3. c
Day 5
 1. B   2. H   3. A   4. G

Week 34

Day 1
 2. d
 3. a
Day 2
 2. b
 3. d
Day 3
 2. b
 3. c
Day 4
 2. a
 3. c
Day 5
 1. B   2. J   3. C   4. F

Week 35

Day 1
 2. d
 3. b
Day 2
 2. d
 3. a
Day 3
 2. b
 3. c
Day 4
 2. a
 3. a, c
Day 5
 1. A   2. J   3. C   4. F

Week 36 Review

Day 1
 located, location, observe, gather, state
Day 2
 requirement, positions, locate, plan
Day 3
 completely, restate, collection, prepare
Day 4
 rules, study, require, complete
Day 5
 1. prepare
 2. completion
 3. statement
 4. examine
 5. collect
 6. observation
 Code: on the bottom